IT'S ALL ABOUT HER

Surviving the Female Narcissist

Lisa E. Scott

E. S. Enterprises

ISBN: 978-0-9858327-2-8

Disclaimer Notice:

Please note the information contained within this document is for educational and entertainment purposes only. Every attempt has been made to provide accurate, up to date and reliable complete information. No warranties of any kind are expressed or implied. Readers acknowledge that the author is not engaging in the rendering of legal, financial, medical or professional advice. The content of this book has been derived from various sources. Please consult a licensed professional before attempting any techniques outlined in this book.

By reading this document, the reader agrees that under no circumstances is the author responsible for any losses, direct or indirect, which are incurred as a result of the use of information contained within this document, including, but not limited to, —errors, omissions, or inaccuracies.

TABLE OF CONTENTS

INTRODUCTION

We are living in and experiencing an epidemic of narcissism. As a result, more and more people are finding themselves in relationships with narcissists. Narcissists are hard to avoid because our culture glorifies their behavior and rewards it shamelessly. Studies show that narcissism is increasing just as fast as rates of obesity in America. Research tells us that today's youth are three times more narcissistic than their predecessors.[1]

I wrote my first book "It's All About Him" after my divorce from a man who is a self-professed narcissist and gave me quite the education on *his kind* (as he would say) to help others recognize and escape the emotional abuse that can occur in such a relationship. I've been amazed by the number of women who have reached out to share their own experience of trying to love a narcissist.

More unexpected, however, has been the overwhelming number of men who have asked that I write about the female narcissist. It's not easy for a man to admit he's been psychologically abused and manipulated by a woman, but such abuse is an unfortunate reality we can no longer afford to deny.

Toxic feminity is a sign of our times many believe. Whether it is or whether we're just finally willing to talk about the fact that women can be just as cruel and even more cunning as men, women abuse men.

We have been conditioned to believe women are nurturers. Women inherently have more empathy and compassion for others because they are equipped to provide primary care and feeding to their offspring, right?

Unfortunately, what is not accounted for in this widely held assumption is the fact that some women experience an *Arrested Development* in their early childhood, which prohibits them from developing or feeling the kind of empathy required to sufficiently care for others. These women suffer from Narcissistic Personality Disorder or what is also referred to as *Pathological Narcissism*, and are incapable of love.

Narcissists seek out relationships to ensure someone is always available to stroke their ego and cater to their never-ending childlike needs. Female narcissists use their physical assets to attract, manipulate and control. While men often use their power and status to dominate, female narcissists have mastered the art of seduction and exploit the fact that many men are visual creatures. They target men they know will have the means to cater to their needs and feed their insatiable ego.

It is often much more difficult for men to spot the red flags of narcissism early on in a relationship. Women can often determine a man's intentions by seeing how patient he is to get intimate. It's not quite so simple for a man. While finding someone of good character is just as important to a man, men are primarily drawn to women via their sexual attraction, which gives an attractive woman a considerable amount of power over even the most discerning of men.

Underneath the flashy exterior of a narcissist is a fragile ego, which requires constant attention and validation. The implications this has on a relationship are far more damaging than one would imagine. Eventually, a narcissist will belittle, criticize, devalue and discard you. This emotional and psychological abuse is inevitable in any long-term relationship with a narcissist. The abuse is not only devastating, but comes out of nowhere and causes you to question and doubt everything about yourself.

Narcissists are incapable of reciprocating love, which makes healthy relationships with them impossible. While they appear caring in the beginning, eventually you realize, they have simply put on an act in order to win and secure your love.

The only reason a narcissist seeks out a relationship is to ensure someone is always present to validate her and indulge her obsession with herself. She has a sense of entitlement that is bewildering. If you want to be in a relationship with her, you should be prepared to provide beyond what is typically considered reasonable. If you don't, she will be sure to remind you that she can easily get this from other suitors in her life with the snap of her fingers. A female narcissist prides herself on having a large circle of admirers (i.e. supply) available to stroke her ego at all times.

"It's a deep and certain truth about narcissistic personalities that to meet them is to love them, but to know them well is to find them unbearable. Confidence quickly curdles into arrogance; smarts turns to smugness, charm turns to smarm."
-Jeffrey Kluger

As I mentioned, my ex-husband was a narcissist. Not just someone who exhibited narcissistic tendencies, but someone who was a self-professed narcissist and diagnosed with pathological narcissism by a certified therapist. Someone's narcissism is labeled pathological when it becomes so extreme they have no ability to recognize other people as independent of themselves. They literally believe the world revolves around them and people exist simply to cater to their needs. It is not just selfish, arrogant behavior that makes a relationship with someone like this difficult. It is much more complicated and thus, important to understand and recognize as early as possible.

Knowledge is power and can be truly liberating.

While my ex-husband joked from day one about being a narcissist, it unfortunately took me many years to look into the true meaning of narcissism and how it impacts a relationship. When I did, it explained everything to me and opened up a whole new world for me. I have made it a goal to share what I have learned with others so they don't live in the dark like I did for years.

While the rise of pathological narcissism shows no signs of slowing down, the good news is you can recover, survive and even THRIVE after narcissistic abuse. Once you learn to see the narcissist for the person they really are, you will begin to free yourself.

NOTHING stands between you and your true self, but the narcissist in your life.

CHAPTER 1

UNDERSTAND IT

Narcissists have often been described as having a Dr. Jekyll and Mr. Hyde personality. Hot one moment and cold the next. You are constantly walking on eggshells worried about what may set them off. They also engage in crazy-making behavior (i.e. gaslighting) to make you feel as though you're losing your mind.

A narcissist has delusions of grandeur that are so severe, it's impossible to live with her and maintain any modicum of sanity. The sense of entitlement a narcissist feels is mind-boggling, to say the least. A narcissist is always right and believes others should feel honored to be in the presence of her greatness.

Narcissists are great actors, which serves them very well in the beginning of a relationship. A narcissist is like a chameleon. She will figure out what you're looking for in a woman and then mold herself into this image in order to win you over.

Once a narcissist has your heart, her true colors emerge and the reality of her true persona can be quite frightening. Once in control, a narcissist becomes demeaning and cruel. She will devalue and discard you within time.

It is critical to your recovery that you understand why the narcissist behaves the way she does. More importantly, you must understand that you have done NOTHING to bring about this drastic change in her behavior. You must accept there is absolutely NOTHING you can do to bring back the woman you thought you fell in love with and adore.

Unfortunately, you suddenly realize this woman never existed. She simply put on an act to win you over.

Accepting this is not easy, but it is imperative we understand this in order to move on. We need to get real with ourselves about what happened in our relationship. Only by understanding the narcissist do we realize we have suffered emotional abuse and trauma at the hands of the person we love.

Narcissists can emulate emotions better than anyone. While they initially appear more sympathetic than the average person, the truth is, they are incapable of feeling emotions. Of course you're probably thinking to yourself, everyone has feelings. You may think that feelings are instinctual and we are all born with the ability to feel. You're right. All humans have emotions. However, everyone is different in how they relate to their feelings.

Humans have found many ways of numbing themselves in an effort to avoid having to feel. For some, drinking alcohol or doing drugs helps numb unwanted feelings and allows an individual to disconnect from themselves for a short while.

Some individuals eventually learn not only how to numb their pain, but develop an ability to disconnect from themselves and their feelings altogether. They separate from their emotions because they have learned their feelings do not help them. They only cause them pain. This describes the emotional state of a narcissist.

One of the most well-known theories in psychology is Sigmund Freud's theory that as children, we pass through different psychosexual stages. According to Freud, if a child is over-indulged or under-indulged in any of these stages, it results in what he calls "fixation." Fixation describes an adult who is stuck or attached to an earlier childhood mode of satisfaction. An infant does not see others as indistinguishable from the self. An infant or small child perceives the world as an extension of themselves. Children feel that people, particularly mother, are present to cater to their every need. They know that if they cry, they can elicit an immediate response in those around them. They will be presented with food and cradling in response to any fussing or crying on their part. They see others as existing solely for their purpose.

This type of selfishness is natural for an infant or small child. They must rely on others to meet their needs in order to survive. According to Freud, this extreme selfishness, or "narcissism," is a normal psychosexual stage of development between the stages of "auto-eroticism" and "object-libido."

Children eventually grow out of this narcissistic stage. They grow out of it and learn to understand that others have needs as well. Unfortunately, not everyone grows out of this stage. If they received too much or too little attention as a child, they become "fixated" in this stage later, obsessed with getting their needs met at all times.

Sadly, a narcissist was either neglected as a child or over-indulged. She is stuck. She never developed the more complex feelings that make us uniquely human, like love and empathy. She does not relate to the world or others in the same way we do.

Recently, many studies on narcissism have found that our modern-day culture is contributing to the rise in narcissistic behavior, leading some to believe less in the theory of childhood neglect or abuse and more in the theory of over-indulgence. Unfortunately, today's society rewards narcissistic behavior over integrity and character.

Those who display haughty, arrogant, self-indulgent and child-like behavior are rewarded with their own television series. Think "Real

Housewives" and "The Kardashians." Our youth have become obsessed with celebrity culture and grow up believing fame is the only noteworthy pinnacle of success.

The self-esteem movement produced a generation of young girls who filled their rooms with "Princess" pillows and participant trophies just for showing up. In fact, 30% of today's students feel they should get good grades just for attending class. Their sense of entitlement is bewildering to professors, which I can personally attest to first-hand as an educator.

Today's social media breeds narcissism by constantly encouraging women to post provocative photos and create online personas that reflect their image. Facebook and Instagram reinforce narcissistic behavior as they require excessive self-promotion. More and more women are becoming addicted to the validation it provides.

Narcissists are obsessed with social media because it provides the ultimate reflection back to them of just how special they are. It acts as a mirror and narcissists LOVE mirrors. Narcissists can often be found admiring themselves in the mirror for great lengths of time.

While one may confuse this for self-love, it is the furthest thing from it. In order to love another person, one must first love themselves. A narcissist loathes themselves down deep. They know there is something wrong inside, but can't figure out what or why they feel so miserable and empty inside.

Bottom line is that a narcissist is emotionally stunted and incapable of feeling the range of emotions, which bring us joy, like love and gratitude. The female narcissist disconnected from her true self a long time ago. I will explain this in more detail throughout my book, but the easiest way to think of her is as a five or six year old child who has yet to understand that she is not the center of everyone's universe. The inconvenient and inevitable reminder that the world does not revolve around her is a disappointing reality she refuses to accept, which contributes to her misery and ongoing unhappiness.

Since narcissists are not in touch with their true self, they are dependent on others to fill a void. Unfortunately, no one can ever fill this insatiable void because their expectations are unrealistic, unattainable and ever-changing. No one will ever be good enough for them and they will repeat this cycle of abusing and discarding romantic partners throughout their lives.

Charlie's Story

Charlie and Monica had been dating close to a year when Charlie engaged my services as a coach. Monica wanted to get married and did not understand why Charlie had an issue with the fact that she needed to have dinner with other men once or twice a week. She told him if she didn't continue to see these other men, whom she swore were just friends, she would feel smothered and stifled by him.

Not only did she expect him to accept this without question, but he was never invited to join these dinners. For almost a year, Charlie put up with Monica going out to dinner in NYC with other men, most of whom she once dated and were obviously attempting to win her over.

Monica had achieved the narcissist's dream of having a rotation of admirers available to her at her disposal and wasn't willing to give it up for Charlie. We often think of men having a harem, but female narcissists are notorious for having a very large circle of men doting on them at all times. When a narcissist gets in a committed relationship, she has a very hard time giving this up and often, as was the case with Monica, may not give it up for anyone.

Today's technological age makes it very easy for narcissists to create a large circle of admirers (i.e. supply). Some create relationships with people in other cities or states because it is very easy to hide a relationship like this from their significant other. I know of many female narcissists who claim to go on business trips only to be found visiting another member of their harem.

Long-Distance Relationships (LDRs) are perfect for narcissists who thrive on having a large source of supply available to them at all times. A narcissist's ego is so fragile that it can never be satiated by just one person. A narcissist requires a plethora of supply and if they're not up-front with you about it, as Monica was with Charlie, they will hide it from you.

Another person often found in the narcissist's "rotation of others" is the online admirer who is even easier to hide and provides just the right amount of ego-stroking when needed. Narcissists often prefer LDRs and OnLine Relationships because they provide validation without much effort and require little to no intimacy, which is something the narcissist dreads.

Narcissists also prefer these types of relationships because they feel it gives them the right to demand lots of sexting. Because narcissists are very auto-erotic, they often find the LDR or OnLine Relationship to be a dream come true. They are easy to hide and require NO intimacy or effort, yet provide plenty of validation for their fragile ego.

Monica wanted Charlie to propose. She had reached her forties and was ready to procreate and behold a mini version of herself. Charlie is a successful attorney who could provide the kind of life she wanted and she knew this. Monica was putting the pressure on to get married, but Charlie was understandably hesitant due to the rotation of men she insisted on having in her life. Ultimately, Charlie ended the relationship because Monica was not willing to give up her circle of men and Charlie knew he deserved more.

Later in this book, I will share first-hand accounts from several others who had a very similar experience, but want to share this brief story upfront as I believe it helps explain the typical behavior of a female narcissist.

I coached Charlie through this break-up and am so glad he stood his ground for what he deserves. Despite knowing in his gut that she was wrong, it took him a long time to fully believe it, which just goes to show how easily the narcissist programs us into accepting way less than we deserve. No one should put up with this kind of selfish and manipulative behavior, but the narcissist is so covert and charming that they are often able to cause us to doubt ourselves to the point that we do accept way less than we know we deserve.

"Never allow someone to be your priority while allowing yourself to be their option." -Mark Twain

There is much confusion and pain when in a relationship with a narcissist. We repeatedly find ourselves let down and disappointed by our partner. We have given our heart and soul to this person, but they cannot return our love and we do not understand why. Often, we deny the reality of our situation for years before we get honest with ourselves.

Getting over a relationship with a narcissist is not the same as with a healthy well-adjusted adult. In a typical breakup, we grieve the loss of love, the pain of saying goodbye, the sadness of something wonderful ending, broken promises and halted dreams.

When grieving a narcissist, this pain is compounded by the reality that this person is not who you thought she was at all. Thinking you know

16) Heightened fear of abandonment

17) Always puts herself first, even before her own children

18) Extremely competitive, even with her own children

19) Very controlling and uses sex to manipulate

20) Exploits others for her gain regardless of who gets hurt

21) Has an addictive personality

22) Often creates drama for no reason

23) Constant push/pull behavior

24) Blames everyone else for her problems

25) Is always right and no one can prove her wrong

26) Projects her issues onto others

27) Manipulates and lies with ease

28) Condescending, demeaning and cruel

29) Unpredictable in her moods and actions.

30) Tells you all of her exes are crazy

Why do they *devalue & discard* us?

Unfortunately, once a narcissist is victorious and secures your love, the idealization phase of the relationship passes and her true colors emerge. You begin to see the pathology of her personality and realize she merely put on an act in the beginning of the relationship to win and secure your love. She becomes demanding and angry, unaware that you have needs or a separate self at all. She simply finds it impossible to see you as an independent entity.

Trying to understand how you went from being idolized and put on a pedestal to being completely discarded is baffling. Suddenly, you can't do anything right and nothing you do is good enough for her. By understanding the inevitable Devalue & Discard (D&D) behavior of a narcissist, you will finally realize what happened and know that you did NOTHING wrong to cause such a drastic change in her behavior.

It's important to understand when in a toxic relationship, you are viewed as nothing more than an extension of your narcissist. Narcissists seek out relationships in order to ensure someone is present to cater to their needs, stroke their ego and make them look good.

Male narcissists often select a trophy wife. Beautiful women are the ultimate status symbol for men...proof of their masculinity and virility. On the other hand, female narcissists are typically attracted to wealthy men who can support their obsession with image and status.

A narcissist will eventually devalue and discard you with no remorse. At some point, she will emotionally and physically withdraw from you and leave you wondering what you did wrong. Please remember, you did NOTHING wrong. It has NOTHING to do with you. A narcissist is unable to attach in a healthy way to anyone. Ultimately, she will pull away no matter what you do.

One person can never fill the deep void a narcissist feels in her life. Narcissists are addicted to and require an ever-changing and dynamic source of Narcissistic Supply (i.e. admirers). No matter what lengths you go to please her, she has a built-up resentment toward you. She knows she is reliant on you for validation. However, she craves variety and is easily bored. As a result, she blames you for tying her down to a monotonous and mundane lifestyle. This creates in her a great deal of anger towards you because she does not want to rely on you, yet knows she must in order to get the validation she so desperately needs. She does not respect you because she knows you put up with a lot of abuse from her. You have done nothing wrong but be overly giving and nurturing. Yet she is angry with you and blames you for all of her unhappiness.

She is urgent, preoccupied with herself and always trying to right her chronic imbalance. While some narcissists are too numb to feel the emptiness in their lives, their behavior causes major suffering and angst among those around them.

Once a narcissist feels she has obtained control of you, you will see a completely different side of her you never knew existed. Once in control, a narcissist becomes demeaning and cruel.

Narcissists are oblivious to others and how their behavior affects people close to them. They dismiss the feelings, ideas, and opinions of others. They are condescending in their nature. They belittle, criticize, judge and put others down.

A narcissist can be blatant about it or quite subtle in her approach. At times, she has a way of putting you down in such a way that you don't even realize you have been insulted until you reflect upon the conversation later or someone points it out to you. Other times, she can be brutally offensive.

While narcissists do not always realize how hurtful their behavior is, it doesn't mean at times, they are not deliberately abusive. A narcissist is purposefully abusive when her relationship with you changes in a way that is not to her liking. This occurs whenever she starts to feel too close to you. Intimacy terrifies a narcissist and she will respond by being abusive in order to push you away.

Another example of when a narcissist is intentionally abusive is if you voice your displeasure or threaten to leave the relationship. A narcissist cannot be alone. She is terrified of being alone and must always have someone present to validate her. By asserting abusive behavior, she is attempting to maintain her dominance and control over you.

A narcissist has a way of turning everything around so you begin to question yourself. She will do something terribly mean or cruel. You will talk to her about it, and by the end of the conversation, YOU are the one apologizing for some reason. A narcissist knows how to manipulate better than anyone.

A narcissist eventually becomes overly sarcastic and belittles you constantly. You begin to feel you can do nothing right in her eyes and your presence is hardly tolerable. You're baffled. You wonder what you did wrong to cause such a drastic change in her feelings toward you. You struggle desperately to return things to the way they were in the beginning. Unfortunately, as hard as you try, things will never be the same again. She is not the woman you thought. It is a maddening and precarious way to live and can drive anyone to the edge of their sanity. When a narcissist feels she is in control of you and is not threatened by any fear that you will ask for too much from her or leave the relationship, she will engage in escapist activity and appear as if she hardly knows you exist the majority of the time. You are merely present to validate her should she not get enough attention from the outside world that day.

You are treated with indifference by the person who once showered you with love and affection. Her "silent treatment" is her way of devaluing you. If you begin to pull away, she will lay on the charm again. A narcissist knows when to engage her false self to ensure you never leave her. She is always reminding you that she understands you like no one else can or ever will. It is essential that she makes you believe only she can understand you. By constantly telling you that you have problems and quirks only she can understand, she hopes you will become dependent on her. By telling you she loves you despite your flaws, she believes you will begin to feel unlovable in some strange paranoid way. This is her way of ensuring you will never leave her. It is narcissistic manipulation at its finest and it is important that you recognize it.

A narcissist will always ensure she has someone present and available to her at all times to validate her. Unfortunately, she will give you no warning when she decides to leave in pursuit of validation from someone new. This is when we must remember we did NOTHING wrong and this outcome was inevitable.

A narcissist will simply discard you when she becomes convinced that you can no longer provide her with sufficient validation. Keep in mind, this evaluation of hers is totally subjective and not grounded in reality at all. Suddenly, because of boredom, a disagreement, an act or a failure to act, she swings from total idolization to complete devaluation.

She then disconnects from you immediately. She needs to preserve all of her energy in order to focus on her new sources of supply. She sees no need to spend any of her precious time and energy on you, whom she now considers useless.

You must accept the fact that you were not an object of love to this person, but a pawn, a mere source of supply to feed her fragile ego; nothing more, but certainly nothing less.

Once you understand how she must constantly change her source of supply, you will realize her rejection of you has NOTHING to do with you. She will repeat this cycle in every relationship she enters. Be grateful this toxic, abusive woman is out of your life and never let her back.

Why can't they change?

People with Narcissistic Personality Disorder are rigid and often unaware that their thoughts and behavior patterns are inappropriate. Research indicates they are rarely the ones who come in for treatment. Instead, the spouse, significant other, children, and parents of the personality disordered are the ones who suffer and seek therapy. Narcissists do not typically seek treatment as they are quick to blame others for their issues.

Furthermore, personality disorders begin in childhood and do not change over time. While narcissists often have a hard time dealing with stress and may have symptoms such as substance abuse or anxiety that can be treated with medication, it is important to understand that the personality disorder itself cannot be treated. These personality traits are so deeply ingrained that they defy change.

One analogy that illustrates the permanence of a personality disorder is to compare it to a mental illness. Mental illnesses (such as Schizophrenia or Bipolar Disorder) can be treated with medication. Most mental illnesses are caused by disruptions in brain cell receptors and synapses, which are believed to be genetically inherited. As long as someone with Schizophrenia or Bipolar disorder is committed to taking their medication regularly, symptoms subside and they feel and act relatively normal.

The onset of mental illness is typically quite sudden and profound. It is often described as though a heavy wool blanket has descended upon a person's personality and smothered it. A personality disorder, on the other hand, is all pervasive.

With mental illness, a person's personality is smothered or blanketed by the onset of the illness. Medication used to restore proper chemical balance in the brain helps to remove the blanket and bring back the true personality of the individual.

In contrast, the personality of someone with a personality disorder is virtually INTERWOVEN into every fiber of that blanket. It is the fabric and foundation of who they are. If you unravel the blanket, you unravel the person's entire personality, which is impossible.

Therefore, the way I see it is simple: you have two choices. You either accept your partner for who she is or you move on. It is critical that you understand you have done NOTHING wrong nor is there anything you can do to change the situation. It is not your fault. You fell in love with someone who is incapable of having an adult mature relationship.

Personality disorders cannot be treated. We must accept the fact that the only person we can change is ourselves. Accepting that there is nothing you can do to improve your relationship with the person you love is painful, but powerful.

Why we must get real to heal?

The painful part is obvious. Loving someone who cannot return your love is agonizing and difficult to accept. However, the knowledge that no matter what you do, this person will never change is empowering, in my opinion. Once you understand this fundamental truth, a whole new world opens up to you. Your newfound knowledge should be liberating.

When in a relationship with a narcissist, we often lie to ourselves in order to keep going. We lie to ourselves that things aren't as bad as they really are. We do not want to accept that the person we fell in love with is not who we thought they were in the beginning. No one wants to admit this. Why would we want to admit this without a fight? We have invested so much in this relationship. We do not want to believe that our soul mate is not real. We would rather exhaust every possibile excuse or explanation we can before we admit this inconvenient truth to ourselves.

I lied to myself for years about my ex-husband, refusing to see the side of him I didn't want to see. Unfortunately, lying to yourself like this forces you to disconnect from your true self just like the narcissist did as a child. Trust me, this is no way to live. Denial is akin to death. When you disconnect from yourself, I believe you die a slow death inside. You become your own worst enemy. Subconsciously, you know you're lying to yourself. You know you are denying your reality, burying your head in the sand and living in the dark.

No matter how hard we try to fool the mind into thinking everything is ok, it knows the truth. The mind is amazingly powerful. We may try to avoid thinking about it by keeping ourselves busy with work or projects. However, at the end of the day, we know we're lying to ourselves.

In order to keep the lie alive, you disconnect from yourself. You then begin to get angry with yourself for not being strong enough to face reality. Anger turned inward turns into depression. So now, not only are you miserable in your relationship, but you feel dead inside, angry and depressed.

"When one is pretending, the entire body revolts." -Anais Nin

We cannot avoid reality. We have to be honest with ourselves. If not, we lose all trust in ourselves. We must "get real to heal," as I like to say. When I finally got real and faced reality, it explained everything to me and gave me a second chance at life and love.

The only certainty you can count on in a relationship with a narcissist is that this person is permanently disordered and disturbed. She will never change. You must accept her for who she is and all her limitations or move on and create a new life for yourself.

I believe in creating a new life. We owe it to ourselves. There is no question that we deserve real and authentic love. Life is short. There are people out there capable of genuine love and we deserve nothing less. In order to receive it, we must first be honest with ourselves about the reality of our situation and face the truth.

Why do they seek out relationships?

So you're probably asking yourself why someone so self-absorbed would have any interest in pursuing a relationship with someone else. What you have to understand is that a narcissist is looking for meaning to fill up her emptiness. A narcissist has no inner sense of self and requires someone prove to her that she exists by reflecting her image back to her.

Narcissists need people more than anyone. They have very specific reasons for being in relationships, but they are not built on the universal need we all have, which is to love. They do not enter or stay in relationships for love. Their motives are quite different. They become involved in relationships in order to ensure their needs are met and someone is always present to provide them with the attention and adoration they require in order to feel alive.

Narcissists feed off of attention. Adoration from others is what fuels them. It is like a drug to them and they are addicted to it. Sam Vaknin, a self-professed narcissist and author of "Malignant Self-Love Narcissism Revisited" calls this drug "Narcissistic Supply (NS)." NS is any form of attention an individual receives from others. [1]

According to Vaknin, there are two types of Narcissistic Supply - Primary and Secondary. Primary Narcissistic Supply is the day-to-day changing attention a narcissist receives from various different people she encounters throughout her day. When a narcissist does not receive enough Primary NS from strangers or others to fulfill her desires, she resorts to what is called Secondary NS.

Secondary Narcissistic Supply is strictly for backup purposes. Secondary NS is obtained from a narcissist's significant other. The significant other is a constant presence in the narcissist's life. Therefore, they are always available and accessible to her, should she encounter deficient Primary NS at some point during the day.

A narcissist needs to ensure she has a constant and reliable source of supply at all times. The best way she has found of doing this is to have a significant other in her life. She does not love this person, nor does she wish to be with this person most of the time. However, because it is impossible to control how much attention or Primary NS she will receive from the outside world on a daily basis, she must make certain she has a backup form of it that is always available to her. It is for this reason a narcissist seeks to find a significant other. She prefers Primary NS because it is ever-changing and dynamic, but when unavailable, she will resort to Secondary NS ... a.k.a. her significant other.

What is the *real-self* vs. *ego-self*?

The following terms have been used interchangeably in our culture for years: real self, true self, inner child, higher self. These terms refer to the same core part in humans. It is who we are when we feel most authentic or genuine. Our true self is loving, giving, expressive, creative, and spontaneous. Overall, we feel whole and alive when we are in touch with our true self. This feeling of wholeness and happiness can only come to us when we are open, honest and real with ourselves. We refer to this as the "Real-Self."

In contrast, what has been called the false self, unauthentic self, or public self describes how we feel when we are uncomfortable or strained. Alienated from the true self, our false self is egocentric, selfish, withholding, envious, and critical. This is what we call the "Ego-Self." The Ego-Self is attached to material things and physical image. The Ego-Self prohibits us from being in touch with our true inner self, which is required in order to attain love and any level of spirituality, in my opinion.

The Ego-Self is often used by individuals as a way to cover up their true feelings. The Ego-Self is inhibited and fearful. Once formed and functioning, the Ego-Self stifles the growth of the Real-Self. The more developed one's Ego-Self becomes, the more nonexistent the Real-Self becomes.

Healthy well-adjusted people engage their Real-Self the majority of the time. The Ego-Self is reserved only for situations in which one feels threatened or uneasy. The Ego-Self is often used as a defense mechanism. The Ego-Self often feels the need to impress others.

All of us are guilty of engaging the Ego-Self from time to time. It typically happens when we're in a stressful situation, nervous or distracted. We just can't seem to be ourselves. We may find ourselves saying something silly to impress someone else without even realizing how ridiculous we sound. It can happen to anyone depending on what is going on in their lives at the time. If we are distracted and not able to focus on the moment, we may try to fill space by saying something without thinking. Bottom line is when we engage our Ego-Self, we are NOT being authentic.

The Real-Self has compassion for others and encourages an authentic interaction where we can truly be ourselves. We are comfortable being ourselves and can drop all defenses. The Ego-Self, on the other hand, has no compassion and refuses to look at reality or face difficult issues.

The Real-Self plays NO role (active or passive) in the conscious life of a narcissist.

A narcissist's Ego-Self has completely killed off her Real-Self. A narcissist is dead inside and will always rely on others to validate her fragile psyche.

The Ego-Self serves many functions to a narcissist, the most important being that it acts as a shield or barrier to anyone who could potentially hurt, upset, or disappoint her. The Ego-Self can absorb any amount of pain. The Ego-Self feels the need to dominate and control, seeing others as nothing more than pawns in a quest for power.

A narcissist typically invents her Ego-Self as a child. By inventing it, she develops immunity to any abuse, indifference, smothering, or exploitation she may fall victim to as a child. She does not want to feel the feelings this mistreatment causes. Therefore, she invents an Ego-Self to protect herself from the pain.

By projecting an Ego-Self to others, a narcissist is able to live in a fantasy world of her own creation. Her Ego-Self acts as a defense shield to ensure her Real-Self (buried deep within) can never be hurt again. It essentially protects her from the pain of her reality. Unfortunately, it also kills her spirit, disconnects her, deadens her inside and prohibits her from attaching to any other human in a healthy way.

Why can't it ever work?

As you now know, narcissists disconnect from themselves as children. What may be even more important for you to understand, however, is not only has a narcissist disconnected from herself, but she will NEVER allow herself to connect with another person under any circumstance.

A narcissist lives in a world of fear. She is afraid of being exposed, afraid of being abandoned and afraid of losing control. Living in a state of fear like this causes her to always be in a "fight or flight" mode. She is always on the defense and unable to let her guard down. As a result, she does not attach to others in a healthy way and inevitably destroys any trust that once existed in a relationship. The demise of a healthy relationship with a narcissist is unavoidable.

Why can't they love?

Narcissists are incapable of feeling love or empathy. It is critical that you understand this. They are stunted emotionally and never developed the feelings that make us uniquely human, such as compassion and love. Healthy, well-adjusted children eventually grow out of the narcissistic stage. They grow out of it and learn to understand that others have needs as well.

Unfortunately, not everyone grows out of this stage. If they were neglected or over-indulged as a child, they become fixated in this stage, obsessed with getting their needs met at all times. This is where the narcissist is stuck. She is stuck at age five and completely oblivious to the fact that others have needs or wants of their own.

The only feelings a narcissist experiences are the primal, instinctive gut feelings we all possess in order to survive – Anger and Fear. We are all born with these instincts as they are critical to our survival.

This also helps explain why when a narcissist becomes upset, she is capable of fierce rage. That's because anger and fear are the only real feelings a narcissist experiences. Therefore, when she feels these feelings, watch out. This is no acting. This is true and authentic rage. While the narcissist experiences these feelings, they do not know how to manage them.

It is actually quite sad. Narcissists are not able to experience the range of emotions we can. They will never encounter pure joy, compassion or true love. Sure, they think they love you but that's because they are dependent on you for survival, not because they are in love with you in any mature, adult or romantic way.

Let me be clear, you did mean something to the narcissist. You made her feel alive. A narcissist only spends time with people who inspire and excite her. However, at the end of the day, a narcissist is incapable of feeling genuine love and will inevitably move on in pursuit of new supply. Her attention is always fleeting and only temporary. She is always looking for the next best high, like a drug addict.

Unfortunately, she cannot help it. Narcissists never develop the complex, evolved feelings that make us human. Deep down they know they are different. They know they should feel these feelings and learn to mimic this behavior by watching others. They do not want to be "found out" so they "act out" the feelings they know they should feel in the beginning of a relationship in order to win your love. Unfortunately, this is only an act and once they feel confident that they have secured your love, their true colors will emerge.

Why can't they accept love?

Narcissists might hope for love and caring, but feel very uncomfortable if they seem to find it. Being in love makes them feel vulnerable and this terrifies them. They doubt the authenticity of real love and devalue anyone who loves them because they believe that person, like themselves, can never live up to their expectations of perfection.

Narcissists cannot grasp the concept of unconditional love that includes the acceptance of flaws. Love does not sustain them. Instead it feels unsafe. Admiration feels safer because it can be earned through achievements and credentials. Since these are things they can control, they feel much safer being admired, rather than loved.

As a result, they seek attention and admiration from as many people as possible. Those who profess their love are eventually discarded and devalued. Narcissists are unaware of how they vacillate between idolizing and devaluing their significant other. At the end of the day, however, it is important to understand:

A narcissist would rather be admired or even hated by many than loved by one.

Why do they dread intimacy?

Narcissists dread intimacy and view it as weak. In their mind, becoming intimate with someone cancels their superiority and demystifies them. They thrive on being unique and in control. In the beginning of a relationship, narcissists use sex as a lure and a hook to reel you in. The art of seduction gives them a thrill and they appear overly-sexual from the high of seducing new supply. They are addicted to it, which is why they are never able to fully stop engaging new supply for the opportunity to flirt and seduce new targets.

Seducing new prey is like a drug to them because it validates their ego and makes them feel powerful and alive. This explains why many people experience a decline in sexual activity with a narcissist once they settle down together.

Are they all the same?

For the most part...YES. Once you understand a narcissist, you can pretty much write the script for the next one you encounter. However, there are some differences worth noting, which may pertain to your narcissist.

In his book "Malignant Self-Love," Sam Vaknin describes two types of narcissists: The Cerebral Narcissist and The Somatic Narcissist.

Vaknin believes when narcissists create and project a false image of who they wish to be, they are either Cerebral (intellectual) or Somatic (sexual). In other words, they either attract attention by applying their intellect/talent or by applying their sexuality/bodies. [2]

Narcissists know by perfecting their looks or exhibiting superior intellect or talent, they will obtain the adoration they so badly crave. Female narcissists are known for using their *physical assets* to lure their victims and men often use their *position of power*.

Once a narcissist determines what they possess that best attracts attention, they will perfect it and hone it like nothing else. They are addicted to attention and will create and project an Ego-Self they are certain will attract the most attention.

The Somatic Narcissist flaunts her body and uses her sexuality to attract others. A Cerebral Narcissist, on the other hand, uses her intellect, knowledge, or talent to attract attention or obtain power.

All narcissists are both Cerebral and Somatic. However, one type is typically dominant in a narcissist. The narcissist may swing between her dominant type and recessive type, but she typically prefers utilizing one over the other.

Cerebral (intellectual) Narcissists regard sex as a chore ... something they must do in order to maintain their source of Narcissistic Supply ... a.k.a. their significant other.

Somatic (sexual) Narcissists derive validation from their sexual conquests. In the dating world, the trend of "hooking up" or sleeping around is perfect for narcissists of this type. They love to brag to others about the numerous admirers they seduce and view sexual partners as nothing more than narcissistic supply.

Another distinction I have seen some make is between:

The Aggressive Narcissist vs. The Passive Narcissist.

The Aggressive Narcissist is one who consciously feels and maintains a sense of self-importance. She knows she is special and demands special treatment from others. She is extremely manipulative and exploitive of others. She can only relate to others who provide her with money, success and power.

The Passive Narcissist, on the other hand, feels damaged and constantly devalues herself. She constantly seeks affirmation from men. She fluctuates between extreme lows and depression where she withdraws from others to an irritable and aggressive mood where she rages and becomes verbally or physically abusive.

The Aggressive Narcissist will only date powerful, successful men and usually plays them against one another in her attempt to determine who is most deserving of her greatness.

The Passive Narcissist is more clingy, but then in an attempt to guard against feared abandonment, becomes demeaning and cruel to engage in a never-ending power play.

How do they *gaslight* us?

Narcissists lead us to believe we have something we actually do not have, and we hold on to it. We think we have a relationship with an amazing person, when in reality we are living with an illusion that our relationship is special. The acting talent these personalities possess is astounding. They are brilliant con-artists and we must accept that the wonderful person we fell in love with NEVER existed. They hid behind a mask of smoke and mirrors in order to obtain control of us and manipulate us to meet their never-ending child-like needs. Once you learn to see the narcissist for the person she really is, you are finally able to free yourself.

The emotional abuse that occurs in a relationship with a narcissist is merciless and relentless. They use several different methods of coercion in order to obtain control over us. They threaten, degrade, shift blame, criticize, manipulate, verbally assault, dominate, blackmail, withdraw and withhold love and affection from us. These are all types of gaslighting.

The term gaslighting was coined in the movie "Gaslight" from the 1940s. Ingrid Bergman won an Oscar for her portrayal of a wife who is made to believe by her husband that she is going crazy and imagining things so he can gain access to her inheritance. He repeatedly lights a gas lamp in one part of the house, causing the other lamps to become dimmer. When Bergman's character asks her husband about this, he denies that it's happening and tells her she is seeing things.

Put quite simply, gaslighting is emotional and psychological abuse. The narcissist denies that events ever occurred or certain things were said.

This causes the victim to doubt what they're hearing and seeing to the point that they begin to question their sanity. A member of our support group was married to a man who would sneak into her closet to tighten the waist line of her pants and skirts to make her believe she was gaining weight.

Over time, the victim begins to believe the gaslighter and essentially succumbs to their brainwashing. They start to think they are imagining things and have some kind of mental illness or faulty memory. When one doubts their perception of reality, the gaslighter is able to control that person because they become completely dependent on the gaslighter for the truth.

Another form of gaslighting a narcissist will often engage in is to project their own behavior on to you or others – a.k.a. Projection. Projection should really be their middle name. They project their behavior onto you in an attempt to hide any actions or truths they do not want brought to light about themselves. It is their hope that by projecting issues of their own onto you it will distract you and others from noticing their malignant behavior.

A narcissist wants you to believe you have problems and issues only she can understand and only she is willing to tolerate. By doing this, she believes you will begin to feel unlovable and never leave her out of fear of rejection in the future.

What are they like with children?

As you now know, narcissists will never let their guard down enough with anyone to ever feel genuine love for them nor do they experience real emotions. Therefore, doing things for others whom they have no feelings for is pointless. Even their own children pose a threat to them. Children talk back and do not always agree.

Narcissists only enjoy being around their children when the child is a shining example of them or when the child does exactly what is asked of them. Since children cannot be on their best behavior 100 percent of the time, I'm sure you can imagine how a narcissistic parent responds to their children on a daily basis.

The majority of the time, narcissists are either jealous of the attention their child receives from their partner and others, or they are frustrated by the amount of time and energy the child requires of them. Since narcissists do not enjoy expending energy or doing things for others unless they get something out of it, they have very little tolerance for the needs and demands of children and resent them greatly. There is no immediate gratification for a narcissist after tending to the needs of a child. Their whole life is about fulfilling their own needs, not others'.

A narcissist's biggest fear in life is to find herself in a mediocre, monotonous existence.

Narcissists feel omnipotent, grandiose, and unique. To live a routine, common, domestic life terrifies them. What is important to understand is that a narcissist will inevitably pull away, disappear or run at some point to avoid the dreaded idea of being settled-down for life.

Unfortunately, when the female narcissist does file for divorce, she often uses her children as pawns against her husband. She sees her children as nothing more than a means by which to tragically torture the man she is divorcing by denying him the right to see his children. The impact this has on the children is devastating. It is hard to believe any mother would put the pathological satisfaction of tormenting her ex-husband before the needs of her own children, but it is an unfortunate reality that many fathers live with on a daily basis.

Why are we drawn to them?

It's easy to fall for them. They are charming, witty and often the life of the party. To spend time with them is exciting and fun. There is an intensity about them that is indescribable. They possess a force that is magnetic. There is simply never a dull moment and they always keep you on your toes.

While it may be easy to see why we're drawn to them, it's worth noting why they are drawn to us. If you're like me, you're an Empath, which describes a person who is highly tuned into other's emotions. I have always been sensitive, and I find this to be both a blessing and a curse. I can feel other people's emotions as if they're my own. I have been told by others that my ability to empathize with them is palpable. While this is a blessing in many ways, it can prove difficult in interpersonal relationships. Empaths feel things more strongly than others and narcissists pick up on the sensitivity of an Empath and take advantage of it. An Empath is the perfect accoutrement to a narcissist.

Empaths are good listeners, naturally giving and always there for people they care about. Narcissists notice this immediately because they purposefully seek a partner who is compassionate and in tune with their never-ending needs. An Empath absorbs the emotions of others and will easily fall prey to a narcissist, who uses others as an emotional sponge.

Empaths are very sensitive to suffering in the world and are often idealists who want to fix the world's problems. Empaths have an incredible capacity for self-sacrifice and are often found volunteering or dedicating time to help others. People naturally feel comfortable sharing their feelings with an Empath because of their incredible ability to feel compassion and connect with others.

Whereas a narcissist does not connect well with others, an Empath connects too much. When Empaths are around peace and love, they flourish. However, when surrounded by an emotional vampire, like the narcissist, an Empath is ravaged. An Empath absorbs the negativity, fear and rage of a narcissist. So much so that they take on these problems as their own and try to fix things for their partner. This is precisely what a narcissist is looking for in a partner and exactly why they seek out relationships with Empaths.

They choose us for a reason. They choose us because we are strong, successful, intelligent and driven. They need someone to take care of them and certainly are not going to choose someone who can't provide for them. They know they can take a lot from us and gain significantly by being in a relationship with us. They want to be taken care of and choose strong people to partner with for a reason. Overall, I believe being an Empath is truly a gift, but we must be careful not to allow others to take advantage of us.

Do they miss us?

As long as a narcissist has someone to cater to their needs and stroke their ego, they do not miss us. A narcissist does not experience emotions the way we do. Our memories are triggered by our five senses. Narcissists have little to no emotion so their memory recall is much different than ours.

There are two types of memory for the same situation. One is explicit memory - a memory of the details of the experience and the other is implicit memory - a memory of the emotions connected to the experience. For example, smelling a baked apple pie reminds me of my beloved grandmother's wonderful baking and brings about an emotional response of missing her. This is what we call implicit memory or emotional memory.

Explicit memory, on the other hand, is different and includes my ability to remember how to make the pie - the details of the experience. Narcissists are very good at explicit memory - the details, the how to, when, where, what, etc. However, they have horrible implicit memory, which is always triggered by an emotion, or sense of smell, touch, taste, etc. They are incapable of bringing forth emotional memories, only factual memories. Therefore, if you wonder whether they have memories of us, the answer is yes and no.

Yes, they remember the details of your relationship with them. However, the emotions of it are totally lost on them. They enjoyed their time with you. Trust me, you made them feel alive. If not, they never would have chosen you. However, they are incapable of feeling any real emotion and certainly will not experience genuine emotions when remembering you. I know it's hard to accept, but it is simply the way they are built.

Why do they *hoover*?

It's important to be aware of hoovering because narcissists are infamous for it even after they abandon us with no remorse. Why? Why do they keep coming back? The narcissist has no inner-sense of self. As you know, they disconnected from themselves a long time ago. Because they have no sense of self, they must be validated by others in order to feel alive. Without outside validation, they feel dead inside.

If a narcissist is feeling insecure or lonely, she will seek out validation from anyone she can get it from. If she comes back to you after your relationship has ended, you must understand she is coming to you because she is not getting enough attention or validation from her current source of Narcissistic Supply. I know this is tough to accept, but it is true. She is not returning to you because she misses you or genuinely loves you. If she returns to you, it is simply because she needs to be validated and nothing more.

According to the online Urban Dictionary, the definition of hoovering is:

"Being manipulated back into a relationship with threats of suicide, self-harm, or threats of false criminal accusations. Relationship manipulation often associated with individuals suffering from personality disorders like Borderline Personality Disorder or Narcissistic Personality Disorder."

The term Hoovering gets its name from the Hoover vacuum. The narcissist uses all kinds of manipulative behavior to *suck you back in* to the relationship. She may threaten suicide saying that she can't live without you. She purposefully plays on your good-naturedness to get you to feel sorry for her.

During this stage, the narcissist reverts back to the initial behavior she exhibited in the beginning of your relationship in order to win you back. She acts loving, compassionate and supportive. She promises you everything you ever wanted and more. She acknowledges the error of her ways and promises to change. Narcissists are very charming so the initial Hoovering stage is often quite successful. Not to mention, the narcissist knows you well enough to know which buttons to push to get you to succumb to her.

Please know that the minute you take her back, she will revert to her old behavior. She is only coming back to you because she is incapable of being alone. She needs someone in her life to validate her at all times. As you will read in the stories shared here, going back never works. Narcissists are incapable of change. No Contact is the only way to go when breaking free.

If she can't get a positive reaction from you, she will ensure she can elicit a negative reaction. This is precisely why she may come back to insult or demean you. All she needs is a reaction from you - good or bad. She doesn't care if it is a positive or negative reaction as long as she gets a reaction from you. She needs to know she still has some kind of hold or effect on you.

Please remember, a narcissist is only returning to get a "quick fix" on her addiction to Narcissistic Supply. She desperately needs outside validation and will do anything to secure it. Whether it be upsetting you to get a rise out of you or charming you into submission, she is determined to get a reaction from you at that moment.

Once you validate her by responding to her in any way, shape or form, she has gotten her fix and will move on to the next best high. Getting a reaction out of you is like a drug to her. She gets off on it and needs it in order to thrive. It gives her a thrill.

Please do not give her this satisfaction. Please do not respond to her Hoovering. The only way to deal with a narcissist is to go "No Contact," which we will discuss more later in the book. Just remember, indifference is the only way to respond to her attempts to get a reaction from you. I hope if you understand why she is coming back, you will be able to stay away from her. Do not give in to her. She is just looking for a quick fix and will immediately move on once she has used you for it.

What is a *trauma bond*?

Many of us don't understand why we can't stay away from them even after we learn how toxic they are to us. We must remember they have brainwashed us. Like a salesman, they keep us coming back with the lure, the promise and the hook.

They are master manipulators. They know how to make us feel guilty, so we will come back for absolution. They know how to make us feel sorry for them, so we will offer to help them. They know how to promise great things, so we will return in hopes that it will be different this time.

They know how to make us doubt ourselves, so we will seek validation from them. Ultimately, they have trained us to return to them over and over again.

There is a principle in behaviorism called "Random Reinforcement," which explains how inconsistent responses to identical behavior can lead to addiction. This same principle is precisely why slot machines and gambling are dangerously addictive. You get a big reward for a certain behavior on one occasion; other times that same behavior leads to a huge loss or punishment.

The thrill that the next go-around might be the big pay-off or reward for a certain behavior keeps us coming back for more. We chase that high from the last time we were rewarded.

Being in a relationship with a narcissist is like a roller-coaster ride with incredible highs and unbelievable lows. It is exhilarating and exciting one moment, and demoralizing and demeaning the next.

We get caught in a cycle of chasing that next high, hoping that if we weather the storm, the next moment will bring the return of the good again. Unfortunately, the good never returns permanently. The narcissist knows by rewarding us intermittently, we remain hooked. They keep us on our toes guessing and always ensure we are left wanting more from them.

Narcissists are brilliant manipulators and know what they're doing every step of the way. They enjoy punishing us more than they enjoy rewarding us. It is all part of a master plan to keep us under their control. Push/Pull is their Modus Operandi. It is part of their lure (the hook) and they use it to play us like pawns.

After spending years with a narcissist, we begin to doubt our ability to make decisions. They have controlled and directed our every move for years. They train and condition us to look to them for answers, which ultimately strips us of our ability to make any choices for ourselves. As a result, we are terrified of being alone.

Stockholm Syndrome is a term used to describe a psychological phenomenon where hostages bond with their captors. The syndrome is named after the Norrmalmstorg robbery of Kreditbanken at Norrmalmstorg in Stockholm where bank robbers held bank employees hostage from August 23 to August 28, 1973.

In this case, the victims became emotionally attached to their captors and even defended them after they were released. The term Stockholm Syndrome was coined by the criminologist and psychiatrist Nils Bejerot who assisted the police during the robbery. Frank Ochberg originally defined it to aid in the management of hostage situations and describes it as: "A primitive gratitude for the gift of life."

There is still debate as to what specific factors contribute to the development of Stockholm Syndrome, but the goal of every abuser is the same – to ensure the victim becomes reliant and dependent on him or her for survival. Continued contact between the perpetrator and the hostage, a long duration before resolution and emotional abuse vs. physical abuse are key components. These are the very components at play when in a long-term relationship with a narcissist, which helps explain why it is so difficult for us to stay away.

Narcissists isolate us from our family and friends so we become dependent on them. As discussed earlier, they use various methods of coercion, including gaslighting to cause us to doubt ourselves and become reliant on them.

Stockholm Syndrome makes it very hard for us to break off contact. Because the narcissist has programmed us to be reliant on them for survival and the truth, we are afraid to be on our own.

This is what we refer to as a trauma bond because the narcissist has conditioned us to believe we can't live without them. The narcissist wants to keep us confused and coming back to them so they can keep using us forever. Once we deprogram from the narcissist, we can break free, which we'll discuss how to do in later chapters of this book.

CHAPTER 2

SHARE YOUR STORY

As humans, we absolutely must process our feelings before we can recover or heal from any painful experience. Until we do this, we remain stuck. This is not only important for our emotional health, but our physical health as well. Research now exists to prove that unresolved emotional pain can cause physical illness.

What we now know is that unresolved emotional trauma floods our bodies with hormones, which leave our immune systems weak and vulnerable to attack. People tell us to just move on and expect us to get over it, but we can't until we fully process how we feel about it, share our story with others who can relate, and organize our thoughts in such a way that we feel we have made sense of the situation. You may ask: "How do I make sense of a senseless situation?"

Well, this is certainly not easy, but I believe sorting out our feelings and organizing our thoughts in a way that helps us feel we have given the experience some kind of form and structure helps tremendously. We have a need to organize the trauma and chaos we experience in life.

It makes us feel better to express ourselves in a way that allows us to finally put the whole crazy mess to rest in our heads. Until we do this, we may always obsess about it. Each of us must find an outlet to give creative expression and form to what we experienced. For me, this outlet has been my first book, "It's All About Him" and a musical album I made with some friends, "Gotta Get It Out."

The key is to find an outlet in which we can express our feelings and share our story. This may include talking to family members or friends, sharing your story in our support group, journaling or creating art or music. Whatever it is, it is critical that you find an outlet to express yourself in a way that helps you release your emotions and put things in perspective. In my opinion, it is the only way to put it to rest in your mind.

A narcissist will never give us closure, but we can help ourselves get the closure we need by sharing our story. Research tells us the main reason for the stress of psychological trauma is that our memories of these horrible events are fragmented. Psychologically traumatic events are ones that have no good explanation. You have painful facts that make no sense, right?

Our natural tendency is to avoid thinking about painful memories or events. We suppress them and hope they will go away. But, they don't. If you don't process them, deal with them and get them out, they will never go away. This is because the mind is most settled when there is coherence to our thoughts.

The only way to resolve conflicting thoughts is by remembering them, processing them and making sense of them. One way of doing this is by sharing our story with others. Sharing our story with people who understand is extremely healing and cathartic. It validates our experience and reassures us that we are not alone in our struggle.

Telling your story allows you to link together your emotional memories, which makes the traumatic events more coherent. It makes memories of these events less likely to be repeatedly called to mind so they can be laid to rest. This stage is imperative before you can move on.

Do not be afraid to get angry… that's your self-esteem returning and you can channel it into doing things for yourself to help you heal. Too often people think anger is a negative emotion. Anger is not inherently positive or negative. It is how we RESPOND to our anger that determines whether it is positive or negative.

We cannot control what happens to us in life, but we can control how we respond to it. Our response is where our power lies.

Taking steps to take care of yourself is a positive response to anger. Do not be afraid to feel your feelings and get honest with yourself. Remember, we must "get real to heal." If you repress your feelings, you will remain stuck. Be gentle with yourself and grateful that you have the ability to feel. When you feel, you know you're alive, right? I would rather feel pain and know I'm alive than feel nothing. The one thing a narcissist can never take away from us is our ability to feel. A narcissist will never experience the range of emotions we do, which is precisely why they are so jealous, envious and covetous of those of us who can.

Today we now have proof that writing is therapeutic. James Pennebaker, PhD., a psychologist and researcher, has conducted studies that show improvement in immune system functioning and emotional well-being when research participants write about difficult or traumatic events in their lives. When you share your story, you no longer feel alone or isolated. You feel connected and understood.

"I will write myself into well-being." -Nancy Mair

As Louise DeSalvo points out in her powerful book, "Writing as a Way of Healing," many writers, like Virginia Woolf and Henry Miller describe their work as a form of analysis or therapy. Before treatment was available, many writers used their work in this way. Writing allows us to release pent-up feelings that otherwise may not have come to the surface by talking. I know this is certainly the case for me. I find writing to be incredibly healing. I love the way DeSalvo describes the therapeutic process of writing:

"We receive a shock or a blow or experience trauma in our lives. In exploring it, examining it, and putting it into words, we stop seeing it as a random, unexplained event. We begin to understand the order behind appearances. Expressing it in language robs the event of its power to hurt us; it also assuages our pain. And by expressing ourselves in language, by examining these shocks, we paradoxically experience delight – pleasure, even – which comes from the discoveries we make as we write, from the order we create from seeming randomness or chaos. Ultimately, then, writing about difficulties enables us to discover the wholeness of things, the connectedness of the human experience. We understand that our greatest shocks do not separate us from humankind. Instead, through expressing ourselves, we establish our connection with others and with the world." [1]

Sharing your story with others in our support group who understand exactly what you're going through is extremely healing. It's comforting to know you are not alone and that others can relate to your confusion and pain. Remember, the narcissist wants us to doubt ourselves and our sense of reality.

By talking to others who recognize the tactics narcissists play, you can help prevent yourself from getting sucked back in by the narcissist. Being connected to others who "get it" is extremely helpful during those times when you are feeling weak and want to see or talk to her.

Write about your relationship with your narcissist. Do not worry about grammar or punctuation. Focus instead on sorting out the series of events in your relationship and most importantly, the feelings you experienced.

"Our story is the medium we use to interpret our life experiences and make sense of them." - **Sandra Marinella**

You can share your story privately in a journal or post in our support group, which you can join using the QR code below:

You will be amazed at what you learn about your relationship with your narcissist and more importantly, your relationship with yourself as a result of putting your experience into words.

Below are additional stories I share with you from members of our support group to show you the importance of expressing yourself through writing and to help you realize you are not alone in your experience.

You do not need to read these stories in order as each is a story in itself that can be read at any time. If you do read some now and others later, please just be sure to read the section titled **Key Themes** before moving on to Chapter three. Please note: all names have been changed to protect anonymity. You will find many offer advice and words of wisdom that come only from those who know first-hand what it is like to try to love a narcissist.

David's Story

I keep saying to myself, "I can't believe it. How did I let this happen?" But I have to believe it, because this happened to me. My narcissist and

I got together close to 5 years ago. The first year was amazing, and the first summer in particular was pure magic. Then she admitted to me cautiously that she had an "anxiety" problem, which had to do with my being away or out of town from time to time. She needed me close, or she would have panic attacks, crying, irrational fear, etc.

Since I'm a decent caring guy and I was in love with her at this point from the wonderful time we had together thus far, I decided to try and work with her on this and that is when the trouble started. She claimed to not be trying to control me, but that she couldn't help having this reaction if I were to go out of town to visit my brother for a few days or if work would call me away.

I am/was a welder, so work was seldom in the town where we lived. I passed up a lot of lucrative jobs so that I could be with her, and commuted to others in nearby towns when I could. If something came up, or I wanted to do something we had to have a plan for her to be without me. I had to give notice of departures - which I began to dread/fear as she would get "into a state" over the potential threat to her world.

At around a year and a half in, I moved into her condo. We would have "practice nights" where I would stay at my parents so she could work on being on her own, in hopes that it could get better.

WOW! I should have run then, but I didn't. I was in love with her. I just wanted to be with her, but she was a great big bundle of need. Gradually, I got isolated from my friends and family, because we had a busy life and "we" needed to do things.

The summer after moving in together we got a puppy, which was another stretch of good times, but after that my life revolved around walking the dog and managing her "anxiety."

She is university educated and has a good government job, while I was a hit and miss construction worker. She started giving me a hard time about not having a "normal job" you could count on, and asked why I didn't already own a house since I was nine years older than her.

I believed she was dropping hints about getting engaged. Mentioning rings, how her friends were all getting married, telling me about how in the long term she needed to be married and didn't want to be "just living together" forever. So, with some serious consideration, I decided that the good weighed more in the balance, and I bought a ring and proposed. Didn't get the joyous response I expected, she had to think about it for a day before she said yes. I've referred to this since as the "shitty proposal." Again, I should have called it there.

The truth was that she didn't want to marry me, knew I wasn't the guy for her in the long term, but that she couldn't bring herself to say no, and convinced herself to say yes. She was trying to scare me off, but it didn't work.

By this time, I was making preparations to go back to school, and spend a few years taking engineering to open myself up to a "normal job" mostly at her nudging, but also I didn't want to be working in the trenches forever either.

All the while, she would keep telling me that I should do what I wanted, and that school should be for me not for her. When an out of town job would come up, she would get on edge, tell me to do what I wanted, but the threat of her reaction was always present.

Two years pass since the engagement, during which I am her rock, her emotional support through two deaths in the family, her father having heart surgery, as well as the day to day trauma, and other difficult events.

I had to spend over a year doing prep courses to get my academic skills up as it had been 20 years since high school. So the year I started the program in earnest, it was very difficult and demanding. The college offering the course is in the city, which is an hour drive away. I have 3-4 hours homework every night at a minimum.

She takes the summer preceding school off from work as stress leave, suffering from the family difficulties of the past few years, and likely from the lie that she has been living for some time now. She starts seeing a psychologist and gets some tools to help with her issues. This seems to have a positive effect and she is diligently doing her "homework" from the therapist to get a handle on things. So I decide that I need to rent a room near the college through the week and would come home on the weekend. We agree to do this and ease into it first a day, then a couple days, etc.

Near the end of the summer, we spent a day trip in the company of this guy she knows through work. For me, it's like tagging along on their first date, obvious attraction and connection between them. I wonder if I'm imagining things, and don't mention it for a few weeks. It comes to my attention that they are walking the dogs together while I'm not around and having tea. So I tell her how I felt on our day trip and that I'm not comfortable with them hanging out alone. Work stuff or a group thing no problem, but explain it's not good that she's engaged to me and he is single. I'm sure you can see where this is going.

So I start being out of town and she keeps hanging out with him. She tells me later that she can't stop because of her anxiety. She's alone and needs company. Of course, I suggest her mom or girlfriends, but that's not good enough apparently. I'm at school and she keeps flirting with this guy.

Short end to the long story is that we agree to stay apart for my last three weeks of school and then we'll sort things out. One week into this she phones me up in a panic, she can't handle the "uncertainty" in the relationship and can she come down to see me the next day to talk? I say no, I'm busy with school and we agreed to stay apart so I can finish. Final exams are one week away and I have all kinds of calculus and physics to do.

We get into it on the phone and I ask her if she is willing and capable of making some significant effort to balance the scales and improve the relationship. Her reply, "No."

Then I say, "Ok, then. We're done, it's over."

What follows for me are two weeks of pure hell trying to keep this in check while I scrape though my classes, which luckily I pass eventually. I come back to the home town and we have a face to face where she is very cool and professional. I vent at her about what I've been put through and say as I have all along about the other guy - that it sure looks like she was aiming for an upgrade. Guy resembles me physically, but manages the engineering office around the corner from the condo, has a house, a dog and is in better shape than me. Hmm? She says strongly that this was never about replacing me. She just can't handle the anxiety - what a load of BS!

I move my things out the next day. She's not there. Considering the way I've been treated, I snoop and read her journal. The only worst fear not realized is that she didn't write about having sex with him, but learned she thought about him for a long time and wondered about the possibilities. She made a list of all his great qualities, the more she sees him - the more she wants to see him. She is "blindingly proud" of herself for finally doing what she didn't have the courage to do two years ago -

say no to the engagement and break up with me. She is relieved that it's over and is excited and optimistic about her new courtship.

Wow, I've been conned. She kept me around for over two years to help with her "anxiety" and family problems. Then at the first opportunity, as soon as I'm used up and unavailable, she jumps at new better supply and manipulates the breakup of us, at the worst possible time for me - on the phone.

I see the little things much clearer now. I see also that it's not anxiety she suffers from. It's just who she really is. The things she says that don't add up, words and actions not coinciding. She will do or say whatever she has to in order to get what she needs, when she needs it, no matter what effect that may have on anyone else.

There's more and more, but this gives you the idea I think. I feel so used and abused and she doesn't understand why I would feel so strongly about this. She "saw no other way out" and in her mind - did what she had to do.

Oh man, how did I let this happen to me? I was strong and self-assured when we met, and little by little I got chipped away, manipulated and maneuvered - then thrown away quickly and callously when I was used up.

Not so bad as some stories I've seen in the forum here, but I'm a sensitive guy and feeling somewhat traumatized. It's been just over a month since we broke up. I'm getting better, but it's hard.

Now she is chasing the new guy hard, planning to lock in her new victim, while I am a 40 year old living like a 20 year old in a ratty basement room near the college and living the life of a broken student. Yeah, she was supposed to back me up with the school thing. I carry her through all those years and then the minute I need something from her, she's out with a new guy.

Bob's Story

I believe my Ex is a 'covert' narcissist - someone who would cover up the arrogance by being the opposite. Yes, I'm a man and it happens to us guys, as well.

She appears shy, like a wall flower. Wouldn't hurt a fly, very endearing, very well liked in our circle of friends. However, we are talking a wolf in sheep's clothing. She has a very highly specialized status job in the city and is EXTREMELY INTELLIGENT. How she works in a team, I don't know. She doesn't really work in a team, actually. It seems like she runs everything, including her boss, and I'll get to the boss later in the story.

I lived and loved her for over 2.5 years. She was never wrong, didn't take criticism at all well. We never argued, which is not good in a relationship and I think this is more of avoidance than anything else. No empathy, no remorse, working always to her agenda, blaming others and failure to take responsibility for her actions.

In the beginning, we were members of the same amateur dramatic group. I liked her. She was attractive, sassy, full of life, etc. We were amongst friends at a pub after a show. She approached me, told me her current relationship wasn't right and she wanted to end it.

In all honesty, she told me about her dodgy past. Now, on my reflection, how much of it was truth or being economical with the truth? Down is up and up is down. She told me she was (and still is) having therapy. Now, there's a thought.

I knew I was taking a massive risk with this person, as she didn't seem to know herself. But in life we take risks. If we don't, we will not know ourselves and remain emotionally stunted. So I went for it and became the new lover or 'source' if you like? She left her partner within weeks so there wasn't much 'overlap' as I didn't want to be the 'other' man. I didn't feel good about myself while we were carrying on, etc.

She moved into a rented a house. I told her, "Have some space. You need time on your own." No. She wanted me now. I was the love of her life, etc. We all know where this is going. She had her house and I had mine, although, I spent all of my time at her place.

The thing is - Narcissists can't stand on their own two feet. They have to have someone. She is so insecure. They have to have a support network. We all need people in our life, family, friends, spouse, etc. but you'll find N's are people junkies. They like to have lots of people that they can tap into and when it ain't going their way, they dump you.

I believe she chose me because, at the time, I was strong. I told her that I was divorced, had managed to sell a very big house and buy 2 smaller houses, one for me and one for my ex-wife and my 3 children. That impressed her. She knew I could help her move on to the next stage in her life and help rebuild her life (i.e. get out of the old relationship, move and buy a house, etc.). I am very good at fixing things DIY and a good organizer, etc. I did an awful lot for her.

MY whole life changed!!! At first, the love, or as I thought it was love, was 'euphoric.' It was just something else. So wonderful. Something I have never experienced before. I felt loved. The sex was just amazing. After a few months (it was a leap year), she asked to marry me.

I was very flattered. No woman has ever asked. I always did the asking and I had only ever asked twice before (1. my ex-wife and 2. one other lover years ago and she said no). Alarm bells were ringing because she had only been out of a relationship for a short while and now wanted to marry me. It all sounds very nice, but a bit juvenile for someone that's 40….but I was so in love…

The first year was great. Yet something wasn't right. IT WAS ALL TOO GOOD TO BE TRUE. It felt like I was dealing with the emotions of a child, rather than an adult. Weird.

Sometimes she would be staring at me (lovingly) and end up walking into something. Always talked of never leaving me. Said we would be together always and forever. Lots and lots of it. Little notes left about the house, saying she couldn't get enough of me. I know that people in love do all this stuff, but it was all so gushing. That's the only way to describe it and I was hooked. This was the idealization stage.

On the gift giving, there were lots of gifts, spontaneous too. I gave back in return lots of love. Love letters, gifts, flowers, etc.

My kids got to know her kids and they all got on great. We had our first holiday together, along with another friend and her children, which now I think was her secondary NS. The more I write about this, the more I understand the nature of the person I was dealing with.

The NS has to be on their best behavior at first. Thing is why did she pick me? She must have had other suitors? I obviously had something that she lacked. She did have pics of friends and family so all seemed normal. Yet no long term friends. In fact, she would criticize them.

Then almost overnight, came the depression, self-loathing and silence. She wouldn't open up or tell me what was wrong. It was like an emotional wall. I felt like I was in the wrong. Perhaps it's me that's getting her down? What can I do to make things better? Why is she like this? Why doesn't she talk to me about what's bothering her?

One thing they are afraid of is intimacy. I mean real intimacy.

She never really talked about real problems with me. She never asked me questions like, "How do you feel about your brother's illness?" or "What went wrong with your other female relationships?" She never suggested we go and see some of my friends in my home town. It was always about her and her agenda. Never about me.

I felt lost. I felt I was changing, disoriented. I was losing my identity. I was so desperate to make this relationship work. I was changing myself into something I thought she wanted me to be.

The sex became less frequent, less passionate and I would always have to initiate it. We never argued. Now, I think she was afraid that would lead to her revealing her true self.

My ex-wife contracted breast cancer. I jokingly said, "Well, we may have to buy a big house and all of us live together, your kids, my kids etc." and I know that scared her.

Intimacy and commitment. An adult would say something like, "Well, I'm not sure if I can do that or I'm not ready for this. Let's talk about this and find a solution," but she didn't.

Can't confront real issues. It's like dealing with a child who isn't getting the right sort of candy. What happens - a tantrum - but she can't have a tantrum because the real person will come out. Writing this all down is helping me make sense of it all.

It felt like she was the flat tire and I was the pump. It was exhausting. On occasions, I would get the blast of something that I had done. Oh my god, when she was angry, you knew about it. Where's the wall flower now?

So now we move on to the next stage-Devaluation. She would dig at me about my age or doing something that was a 'dad thing' or undervaluing my achievements. It came from no provocation, whatsoever. No matter what I did to try and please her, it wasn't enough. I felt like I was becoming a person she wanted me to be. I was going insane. It was give, give, give and nothing coming back. So I tried to detach myself albeit, for my own well-being.

Then came the Discarding.

One night, she just dumped me. No explanation, nothing.

"We have no future," is all I got from her.

I was devastated. There was no closure.

I had no contact with her for 8 weeks. Then we met in a pub by accident and she told me that she still loves me.

"Let's try and patch things up," she said.

And like a mug, I tried. God did I get the runaround. Only to find out, after a few weeks at trying to 'patch things up' and make some sense of the past 2.5 years, that she's now found the love of her life and it's her boss that she's worked with for 13 years. He has left his wife. She (my exN) loves him, but he doesn't know it. Yeah, right. She is a good liar.

She has done this cycle of partners 3 times, including me as far as I know. All with overlap, basically forming the next relationship before ending the last one. And then, strings me along in case it doesn't work out, she'll carry on with me.

Now there's no contact and there never will be. I've had a lucky escape, but at a cost. I am in my recovery mode at the moment, but each day gets better.

Conclusion - The Narcissist:

- Feels entitled to do whatever they like
- Uncaring (may show that they care, but if it has no benefit to them, they don't care)
- Fears abandonment
- Cannot stand on their own 2 feet
- Feels superior, above everyone else, including you
- Idealization. Always looking for the perfect lover or scenario
- You - the NS - will always be 2-3 steps behind
- Be thankful that you are acknowledged - even just for now. Nice, nice person
- Controlling
- Lacks empathy
- Feels little or no remorse
- Not in touch with themselves
- No sense of identity
- Can't take criticism well
- Never wrong
- Avoids confrontation
- Seeks absolution in the abused partner
- Economical with the truth
- Lying and will distort the truth so they look good and they believe it to be the truth. You challenge the lies at your peril
- Secretive
- Works to their own secret agenda
- They only feel fear and rage
- Fear of intimacy
- She had a particular fear of snakes...hmm perhaps she's seeing something of herself
- Will only do something that benefits themselves
- What they are looking for doesn't exist
- Therefore YOU no longer exist

- As we know, they need to look inside themselves which they will never do

Sad really, as there is no happy ending. On a positive note, I always look at my cup being half full, rather than half empty. I always look to gain from an experience, rather than lose.

To help get over it, write down your story. You will realize, you're not alone. Other people have similar stories. This is your story - and in fact, treasure it. Add to it, craft it. It's you now and it's time you nailed this demon and put it away forever.

The N has given you a gift by stripping you away - you now have a chance to rebuild yourself into a better person. Seize that chance, because believe me, you can change yourself for the better. I know I have. You will feel better in time. Believe that you can be happy again. You don't need ANYONE to validate who you are. Believe in positive karma. Believe in yourself. I know I am a good person. I am valued, loved and understood by those around me.

The narcissist isn't any of these. They've denied themselves of it and it's not through choice. I think it's wrong to belittle them. It might make us feel better in the short term but in the long term it doesn't. They are tortured infantile souls that will never grow up, because quite simply, they can't. In my case, I think her mother is a narcissist as well. Her mom is on her own and has been for years. She gets her NS through her kids and grandchildren I think. And to add to the irony - my exN has said she will probably end up like her mum – alone. How prophetic or should I say pathetic?

Frank's Story

I was in a relationship with my ex for over 1 1/2 years. We have been broken up for seven months now. This whole time I've been trying to reconcile and get the relationship back. I had no idea I was dating a narcissist until recently by doing tons of research and finding out what one was. I HAD NO IDEA I WAS FEEDING THE BEAST AND GIVING IT EXACTLY WHAT IT WANTED!!!

In the beginning, everything was perfect, just like everyone says. Then slowly, a dark cloud rolled in and everything went to hell. At first I thought we were just having some problems with communicating. Then it started to get worse and worse. She started to not care about any of the concerns I had in the relationship. They were all just my problems to her. She would never ever show any empathy towards anything or just a little to keep me guessing. I think this is when the mind games started. One minute, the girl I loved from the beginning, then the next, this careless monster.

I honestly had no idea what was going on, but continued on with her because I loved her very much. I was under her spell. There was also constant lying about talking to ex's from her past, which she told me they would just not stop calling her. I believe now this was a complete lie. I know now that they were part of her supply that she couldn't let go.

Eventually, at the end of the relationship she went out of town. I completely trusted her still. Later, I found out she met up with her ex. Finally, after two weeks of her return thinking everything was fine, she broke up with me. This completely screwed up my head. She started to blame the relationship ending on me. Everything was my fault for the first month. I tried relentlessly to get her back. Then I stopped calling for a week, trying to go No Contact. I wasn't strong enough at the time she called and you bet I answered. This would be the first of many times this happened.

I honestly thought I could get her back with being the best possible guy. The guy she praised in the beginning. All the while, I was just giving her the cake so she could eat it to. She lied to me even more and more and I believed every bit of it. She would call, I would answer, listen to her talk about everything she wanted, but when I started to talk about me or the possible future of us, she didn't have time to talk anymore. She just kept me on the phone long enough to keep me wanting more.

She would finally agree to meet up. We would have what I thought would be a good time. She would come home with me and then in the morning, she would completely change who she was from the night before. She said it was a mistake and made me feel like I tricked her into being there. Always putting me down to make me feel horrible. That's exactly what I let happen for seven long grueling months. All the while, lying to me about everything from seeing other guys, which I didn't want to believe, to telling lies about me to her friends and family without me knowing.

It seems now from what I've found out with all of this is that this was the plan all along to hook me in and make me think that I'm the only one, all the while lying and manipulating me. Then when she was done, to discard me and just keep me on the back burner as one of her supply sources. Well, this last month I've caught on. I had enough. I tried to tell her no more. I need to know what's going on. I can't do this anymore.

Then she brings out that she misses me and wants things how they were and remembers all the good times of our relationship. She says she's not opposed of us getting back together. We just need to work at being friends first. I believed every word of it too. She even asked me to write her parents a heartfelt apology letter for the times I might have been a jerk. I did have my moments because I was going completely insane at some times trying to figure out what was going down. It's extremely hard to see through their lies and maintain your sanity with these types of people. So that's what I did. I wrote her parents the heartfelt apology. I gave it to her that night at her house and she said that this will be really good and will help things out.

I waited two days to contact her to see how it went over. When she answered the phone she acted like she didn't know me. The conversation was as if she never asked me to write it and that she wasn't really concerned about it. She didn't have time to talk about it and I was bothering her because she was getting ready to go out for the night. That moment is finally the first time in over almost 9 months that I felt like I had my balls back. I was so ANGRY AND PISSED OFF about being tricked again into actually believing her. I absolutely went crazy. I told myself that I was gonna find out every lie and manipulation she has said and done to me and confront her about it just so she can feel the same hurt and pain that she put me through.

That was the worst thing I could ever have done. I should have cut my losses a long time ago and said good bye at the initial break up, or at least at that moment, just walked away. I didn't though. I proceeded to find out what was going on, which in turn hurt even more because the lies I found out she had been saying and the things she was doing destroyed me. It made it 10 times worse. It built me up with so much anger and resentment towards this person that could care less about me. I did not know what I was going to do, but I knew I had to release it.

So last Friday, I went to where she would be at and confronted her. First, I asked a question that I wanted to see if she would lie about, which she did. Then, I asked her others......more lies, all while having a smile on her face. Then, I began to tell her how I know she's lying, how I can see right through her, and that I want nothing ever to do with her ever in my life. I told her she is a shitty person and by this time I am yelling at her, trying to make her feel horrible. Still, she has a smile on her face, which just made me even more upset. I began name calling her before I finally left.

Later that night, I went and got drinks, a habit that I picked up through all this turmoil. I started to try and get her on the phone by calling probably a hundred times and sent tons of text messages all during that night, just hoping she would feel a little bit of how I felt the past months. I wanted to get even, to finally have my closure, and I thought I gained the upper hand again by telling this person off.

Wrong, dead wrong! Monday morning, I wake up to a police officer at my front door serving me injunction papers from her. After I left, she called the police and said that I harassed her and that I put my hands on her. She has text messages from me and voice mails, which were definitely angry from me confronting her from all the past lies and manipulations; and from her making me her puppet, or myself allowing her to make me her puppet. Worst idea ever! I should have known better. Now I am so scared about this court hearing and what possible things she could say to the judge to make me look horribly bad; or what lies she's already been saying to people over the past months that I don't know about. I never called the cops on her when she was going crazy so I have nothing to go on.

Joe's Story

We met 10 years ago. She was, I'd have to say, the most beautiful woman who ever fell (so I thought) head over heels in love with me.

"I really don't want to be without you for one minute," she would say. The first time we spent the night together, she cried and cried.

"Why are you crying?" I asked.

"There's nothing wrong with crying," she replied.

She moved in, with her little dog, cleaned my place from top to bottom, had me working out, eating healthy, and in general, we had a lot of fun together.

There were upsetting things. She was the worst backseat driver in history. I would have to get up at 4:00 a.m. in the morning to get her juice. I'd bring the juice back, and she'd say, "No, too sweet, put some water in it."

Nevertheless, I felt so lucky that a woman this beautiful was so into me. I gave her an engagement ring. The landlord said that the dog was not allowed, and we would have to find another place. So I went looking for another apartment and found one for $200 per month more.

Since I was paying the entire rent, I asked her to kick in the extra $200 per month. She said no, and it was at that point I realized I wouldn't be able to continue with this relationship, as it was too much of a drain on my finances.

She moved into another place and I left the state to take care of my aging parents. I paid half of her rent for the first six months on the condition that if I needed to come back and visit for business, I could stay there. I believe I only went back one time, and eventually it ended.

Fast forward 5 years and I get an email from her. She is pregnant and asking if there is any way she can come stay with me for a while? I balk, because I would not like to come in the way with her and whoever the baby's father is, maybe they can work it out. She never does come, but sends me a pic of the beautiful new baby. I send her a gift certificate and that's that.

A few years later, we reconnect on Facebook. I haven't actually seen her in 7 or 8 years and yet I am amazed at how good she looks, even better than before, and she is now nearing 40. She had cosmetic surgery (breast augmentation and nose job) done and her daughter was simply beautiful as well. So we exchange pleasantries back and forth. I don't really know if she's dating or what she's into.

Then I sell my house, business, etc., and move to NYC with a small nest egg. It had always been my dream to live and work there. We start getting a little more intense on Facebook, and I invite her and her little daughter to come and see me. Eventually, she agrees.

"Can I bring my nanny?" she asks. I tell her no, explaining that it would cost a lot, and I have a small Manhattan apartment.

So, she comes. Oh my gosh, what fun. We didn't even explore the city that much. We just had fun with each other and her adorable little girl. They stayed about 4 days, and when I sent them in the car service for the trip to the airport, I walked back into my prized NYC flat and experienced some of the most intense longing and loneliness of my life.

I said to myself, "Why was I so resistant to being with her 10 years prior? Why wouldn't I just be happy to be with a beautiful woman and if she wanted her juice less sweet at 4am, just get it for her?"

Turns out she was seeing another guy. Nothing serious, she says, but yes, she was.

I ask, "Why would you come out here to see me if you were already with someone else?"

She says, "It's not a big hot heavy romance and besides, we were just old friends catching up."

So I put on the full court press. I start sending gifts, flowers, etc. I try to get her to move to NYC, but she says no, she won't do the cold weather.

She suddenly says to me, "My baby is growing up so fast. I want another one. I want to be pregnant right now."

I respond, "You can't tell me that and still be with this other guy. I love you." She finally agrees that she will end it with the other guy and I move to her.

I say to myself, "OK, this is a big risk, but this is it, my best chance at love."

Age and motherhood seem like they've mellowed her out and I'm more ready for it as well. So I sell everything I own, take all the cash I have with me in the bank, get out of my hard fought lease and relocate.

The small nest egg I brought with me is evaporated in 4 months and something else happens as well. She is an entertainer. She never really had that big a career and I figured that she is about done with it and ready to concentrate on family and our own business.

Now there were narcissistic traits I uncovered with her the first time. But a) I didn't understand narcissism and b) I really thought the child and getting older would ease it.

Wrong! A sudden burst in her popularity made things worse. Suddenly, all the plans we had made were out the window. She couldn't get pregnant because of her new gig.

She wanted me to come to every single one of her shows, which was ok, except she didn't leave after the show was over. She would stay around for an extra two hours and soak up all the attention from the (mostly male) fans.

When I went broke so fast, I thought, "Well, she's probably going to dump me now."

My business is seasonal and we had to endure about 3 months of very little funds before a significant cash flow would come in. We had to send the full-time nanny, which I paid for home and I became the nanny. Of course, nothing was ever done the right way.

She would say, "Why do you make such a mess. Why don't you clean up as you go?"

I said, "Well, when you're in a rush and you're getting ready, you leave a mess too."

She replied, "Yes, but I have someone to clean up for me."

It was such a rough 3 months. One time, I messed up (i.e. didn't tell her where I was for 2 hours) and she yelled at me non-stop for 5 or 6 hours. Over and over. I got extremely defensive and lied to her and she could sense I was lying. Finally, I went back into her room, and said, "Look, I'm not going to live with someone I feel I have to lie or hide stuff too. Yes, I made a mistake and this is what I did."

That didn't help. She continued to escalate and it got worse and worse. I said, "Forget it. If this is the way it's going to be, I'm going to leave."

She started to cry a bit with what I still believe was true emotion because she was holding the tears back. I realize she had serious abandonment issues and I felt so bad. I made up my mind then and there that no matter what she put me through, I would hang tough, especially for the sake of her daughter, who I was very attached to.

There were so many guys after her - rich ones, powerful ones, and famous ones that she started looking heavily behind my back. One particular guy, a real "nice guy" type who inherited a large family business and who was flirting with her since right after I moved there, caught her interest and all of a sudden, her FB got locked away and the phone never left her side.

Business started picking up so I was working a lot. When the money started coming in, I set down boundaries. She wanted access to the bank account and I said no. I stopped staying out at her shows because I had to get up early to work.

And sure enough, eventually, she didn't come back. Two nights she spent out with this guy, twice in two weeks. The second time, I texted and said, "I was planning on going away this weekend, but I can leave right now if you want?"

No response. So I packed up my stuff (all clothes she bought me after she threw out all of my clothes), which fit nicely in my car and left.

It's funny because I can remember praying to be out of the relationship. When I left, not knowing where I was going, actually, I felt so free. But then it hit me, and I felt crushed.

She blamed me for leaving. She said, "You were always threatening to leave, and you did. We're done. It's over."

I drove by her house the next morning, saying to myself, "She wouldn't. There's no way she would." And sure enough, there was his car.

So she was simultaneously sleeping with my replacement, while blaming me for leaving, even though her staying out all night with the guy was the reason I left!

I begged. I pleaded to get back with her. She was cold and heartless. When she did come and see me at a gig (I was so surprised to see her) she bullied me, told me to shut up, told me there was no chance we would ever get back together, told me to go see a therapist, that it was done, finished.

I asked, "What about your child? Can't I see her?"

"No," she said.

It was then that I realized if it ever came down to a contest between her happiness and her child's, hands down her happiness would win and she would rationalize it by saying, "Well, if I'm not happy, she won't be happy either."

Andre's Story

I wasn't married to her. I don't have kids with her. None of that. I should actually consider myself lucky compared to a lot of people here, who were physically abused by their partners, financially stripped down or what have you. I had none of that. All I have left are memories of amazing moments, combined with those where I felt someone was sucking the life out of me. A lot of people tell me "Andre, you dodged a massive bullet the day you left her."

So why do I feel compelled to share my story?

Well, because every, and I mean, every sign of narcissism was right there before my eyes and I simply didn't know what it was. I couldn't piece things together because I was in love and extremely confused.

The interesting part, I think, of this story, is that you get to see the gradual unveiling of the narcissist and how it went from "Perfection" to "Hell." From little lies to big lies. Some of them, extremely ridiculous.

So here we go:

I am a 29-year-old guy, living in NYC, and from Portuguese background. I am doing pretty well in my career. I have what some people say an interesting life. I live between NY and LA and get to meet very interesting people for work. I can't say my life is boring and I have had my fair share of women. I thought I had "met every possible kind." Well, that was until I met my very first narcissist, during a holiday in Lisbon.

I saw her and instantly connected with her. She was gorgeous, funny, and quirky. Thin, long hair, green eyes and a killing smile. She had undergone breast plastic surgery a couple of months before I met her. Well, long story short, she was perfect. I have met gorgeous women, but there was something about her, something hypnotizing. I immediately fell in love with her within a matter of days. The connection was immediate. The level to which we established immediate "intimacy" was beyond surreal and so was the sexual chemistry.

We could spend hours and hours in each other's company and talk. She would make me laugh like no one else. She was feminine and had an amazing sense of style. Everything was there to be perfect. She told me of all the men she had been with, I was by far the one she truly felt a genuine connection with.

Being with her was the best possible feeling ever. So we decided to try long distance, given that we would see each other every month for about a week. We thought, "Let's start from here then we will see how it goes." I was working remotely from Lisbon for 2 months so we ended up spending a lot of time together at the beginning and thought the long distance was worth the shot.

But then some things started to throw me off, that's where the "fun" part starts getting... well.....not so fun.

First, she would never ever pay for anything. She wouldn't even pay for a cup of coffee! Literally, nothing. Whenever I wouldn't pay for her, she would get immediately passive aggressive. During New Year's Eve, we were having dinner with friends and I paid for her dinner. She didn't say a word. That's when I voiced it and said, "You could at least say thank you for dinner." She responded by flying into a massive rage.

For the first time in my life, I saw real animosity in someone's eyes. And believe me, I am in no case an "innocent guy" or the all-around "Nice Jo." I have values and character, but that threw me off. That was a first red flag. During dinner, she wasn't paying a lot of attention to me and was obsessing over taking pictures (a lot of pictures) with her other girlfriends.

As we leave dinner, we are waiting on a cab to come pick us up and I ask her, "Do you have money to pay the ride?" and she tells me, "Yes, I do." I tell her, "Make sure you have since there is an ATM right behind you." She didn't check her wallet.

We take the cab, go to the party and as he drops us off I look at her, expecting her to AT LEAST pay a cab ride. She tells me, "No I don't have money and I wasn't about to walk on the pavement with high heels, which is why I didn't go to the ATM."

The next day, we go visit an old castle outside Lisbon. As we reach the entrance, I tell her, "You are paying for this one." She didn't say a word, but again, I could feel something mean in her eyes. She wasn't talking to me. Anything I would say would be shut down immediately.

One time she was visiting me here in NY. Again, not one single dinner was paid. When I was not next to her she would go mad. I had to work and couldn't take days off to be with her (before she came, I told her it would be difficult for me to take days off).

When I wasn't with her, she would hate text me for not being with her (again…I was working). I always remember this time when I ordered some food (it gets funny), a Chinese chicken with vegetable. She grabbed the food, while I was still in the kitchen prepping some stuff, and she ends up eating all the chicken and left me with only the vegetable.

She was also constantly asking me to take pictures of her, everywhere, at any time. She would "pose', pretend she was looking at the sky, and display a "fake smile" to look good. We would go out for dinner and instead of having a conversation, she would be on her phone, checking all the pictures I had taken of her during that day. She would try all different sorts of Instagram filters to see which one would make her look best. That's when I realized this was not going to last. I barely saw her and when we were together, she was more interested in her pictures than in us!

But I still loved her, and right before she left NY, she took me to Central Park and told me, "I would like to tell you something I never told anyone before. I love you. From all my heart, I love you."

But after that trip, I decided that we were through and that's where I made a huge mistake. I still kept in touch with her, but I let her know that I wasn't feeling comfortable pursuing the relationship. I was making a career change and was too focused on that. I continued to text her.

When I told her we were done, she said I had abandoned her and that she was willing to go to the end of the world for me. She told me she would live in a slum if need be, as long as she could be with me. All she wanted was to be with me, take care of me and be next to me. No one had ever told me that before... and well... I believed it.

A month goes by. I had a trip planned to Miami for a week with two friends. Turns out she was also on holiday during that week, but I didn't invite her to come. In my mind, again, I knew it was over and I needed to move on, despite all the love I had for her.

She continued to tell me that she loved me and she missed me. Two weeks before the trip, she texts me, "Hey, I thought I would let you know that I am getting married." And that's when my world collapsed.

I was still feeling so much for her. She was telling me two weeks before that she loved me and now she is getting married?? I asked her why she would tell me she loved me if she had someone else. Her answer was, "You didn't want me. I was willing to go anywhere for you, I was ready to move to NY, but you didn't want me."

So then I thought, "Andre, you are making a huge mistake by not giving this a chance. This woman is ready to build something with you, and you are being focused on your career, and probably missing out on something."

What an idiot I was to think that.

So I text her back, "Come join me in Miami and we will see if this is worth trying." She tells me that she will break the engagement because I am THE only man she loves and will always love.

I go online, get her ticket (what a moron), and we all meet in Miami the following week.

That's when Sh** hit the fan again.

The second night, I had a chat with her and said, "So if you say that you are willing to move to NYC, I am willing to give this a chance and build something solid with you."

I told her if she was to come, she would need to find a job and that I wouldn't live with her right away. Rome wasn't built in day and things take time. She said she agreed and that she would move because that is what she wanted - to be with me forever.

Well… words, words, words.

She was COMPLETELY obsessed with herself during that holiday, constantly taking pictures of herself (over 700 pictures of her ONLY in about a week). She would never ask to take a picture with both of us. When I would not pay attention to her, she would go bezerk again and at the same time she said she would be willing to follow me to the end of the world. I remember one night, we came back from a club, she put on a swimsuit at 2.30 a.m. and asked me to go take pictures of her in the pool. Yes, that happened as well.

We barely had sex during that trip. She was always finding an excuse - she was too drunk or she was not feeling well or what have you. She told me, "I was engaged with someone up until a week ago. I can't just switch like that. You need to give me time."

Turns out that engagement was all lies. One night she forgot to close her email, and while she was under the shower, I went in her mailbox. There was absolutely nothing related to a wedding or engagement. No emails at all about it and she keeps all her emails. Her fiance's name supposedly was Filip and there was not one single email from a Filip.

She was a disaster. I would take her out for dinner and not one single thank you. One night, one of my friends treated us to dinner. When I asked her if she thanked my friend, she raged like never before, saying I had received a poor education and that I was an idiot for lecturing her on how to behave.

Anyways, after that trip in Miami, I told her, "We are done for good now. This is pointless and we have different values." She kept telling me I was the man of her life bla bla bla. This goes on for about two weeks after that trip.

I remember her texting me on a Friday, "I am sorry it didn't work out in Miami, but it is because we were with your friends. We had no intimacy. I love you."

This was all lies. We spent enough time, she and I, but every time, she was more interested in taking pictures of herself or checking her Facebook, than to speak with me.

So this was on a Friday. Then two days after, on Sunday, she texts me to say, "Hey I just thought I would let you know, I have committed to a new relationship. :) I still love you very much."

I just answered by telling her goodbye and that was it.

I no longer had her on my Facebook, but I was too tempted to see and I realized that she had changed her Facebook profile picture to be with this new guy with a big heart as a caption. I only had her on my Whatsapp and "by some miracle" she also changed her Whatsapp picture to be with this dude she just met, as if she wanted to rub it on my face. I blocked her from Facebook and I noticed she removed that picture. When I unblocked her, she put it back. I had to test.

One night, I was drunk and went to check her Instagram (Rookie mistake) and saw she was still posting pictures of her in New York and Miami, during OUR holidays, and she has a new boyfriend. She posts pictures of things she and I used to do, but now she is doing them with him. She is obviously trying to get my attention. She would never post anything before and suddenly she wants to come across as the happiest girlfriend in the world.

She still tries to get my attention here and there by commenting on posts on Facebook with the only friend we have in common. I wonder why since she has a new narcissistic supply source. She is manipulative, but I won't write back or even react.

Yes, I miss the good times, but I have to accept the fact that this was all a "mirage." Live and learn. I feel empowered to dodge the next bullet, should a narcissist try to shoot me down.

Jim's Story

I met my NPD girlfriend on a dating site and we were together for 9 months total. The romance moved very quickly in the first few months. She made me believe I was the best boyfriend she'd ever had. She was constantly saying, "I love that about you" and promising me the world. She promised we would start a new business together that would take care of my debts (her idea). She plugged right into who I was.

Then 3 months in, things started to slide. At first, we would fight every second weekend. Then every weekend. Always about how I wasn't "responsible" enough, even though I was working day and night on my job and business. She called every day and interrogated me about how and why I was doing things. Then we went camping and she got drunk and threatened to throw herself from the moving car while screaming what a loser I was.

At that point, I said we couldn't go on until we went to counselling. She agreed. We went to one session and everything went ok for a few weeks. Then the insults started again and worse. No-win situations. Gaslighting. Bike rides with exes, etc. Every promise was broken. Finally she exploded at me while drunk at a party. I left devastated and we broke up the next morning.

A week later, I started missing her and decided there were things I could have done better to make her happy. I called her and admitted my faults and we agreed to get back together. She said she thought I was a lost cause and was glad to hear I'd matured and came around to her way of seeing things.

HUGE MISTAKE. For the next month she treated me like I was on probation and not really her boyfriend. During the last week she was basically screaming at me non-stop (when she did talk to me). Things like, "All you do is d*ck around getting your haircut and going to the dentist" (which I'll admit I did do that day). I kept saying sorry and trying to make it work until she finally had a meltdown and stormed off. She called me later that night drunk and slurred, "I'm sorry you couldn't grow up" and hung up.

At that point I accepted it was over. Nine days later she texted to apologize, except her apology basically said, "I'm sorry for not acting with grace, but I was stressed out trying to make things work with you. I loved you with all my heart and always will. You're a wonderful guy just the way you are. I'm sure you'll find someone who's on board with the way you want to live your life."

I responded that there was, "No excuse for her behavior and that I had loved her as best I could. No one is perfect. No hard feelings."

She said, "I was just trying to apologize. Fine, I'll never contact you again."

It's been 2 1/2 weeks since the texting and a full month now since she stormed off. I've been in therapy every week and am feeling better slowly.

Victor's Story

I established No Contact, blocked phone and email, contacted police with a trespass notice ready to go and went a whole week without hearing anything after having been harassed. Then I got a letter, a confession of her wrongs but somehow managing to put the blame on me. I ignored it, put it in the cupboard with all the poems, photographs, gifts etc. she gave me during the first stage of sweetness and light.

A week later again, I got another letter in the post. This time, a card with a child's drawing of a butterfly on the front, endearing, using all the sweet names she used to call me, drawn sad faces - all of it targeted at my emotions, I suspect. I figured she was trying to reel me back in again. She said she wanted closure after shouting over the top of me every time I opened my mouth to speak, reason, reconcile and after hanging up on me on the phone before I could get a word in.

I took a shower and had a think about it. The timing was spooky, uncanny - I'd just reached the stage of raw disappointment, after feeling really angry for the way she treated and used me, and then after a phase of feeling sorry for the child she must have been once and what that child must have gone through. I was emotionally abused as a child myself, but had reached a stage of trying to heal and move-on, or so I thought.

It wasn't that I wanted to see her again or was it, really? I decided the only way we could progress was if she was willing to admit to her pattern of sadistic abuse and manipulation, which she carried out in a 'covert' way, under her mask. I knew in my mind that, being a narc, she'd NEVER be able to do that. I rang her up and she said she'd been really sad getting over us. I told her I doubted that. I arranged to meet her in the park - a public place. Having acquired insight into our relationship and knowledge about narcissism, I felt strong enough to deal with her. I even took a Dictaphone in my pocket and recorded our conversation in order to defend my sanity against any future attempts at gaslighting.

Anyway, we met. I told her about her abusive pattern, etc. She just listened, mostly. When she tried to defend herself I just kept on track, didn't let her divert, and didn't let her deny what really happened. Now I was feeling powerful. I felt like I was finally overcoming her, standing up for myself. Proud I was keeping my cool and keeping reason and sense on track.

When she asked for more examples of this abuse I was speaking of, I mentioned one of the times she used sex to coerce and degrade me. She told me I had my version of events and at that point she broke away, wouldn't listen anymore, and wished me well. I wished her well too and just walked away, left her standing there. Take that, Narc!

Then I got home. I was thinking about her all over again, of course. Then a few hours later the phone went. She was in tears. She said she was going to start counselling and that having come out of an abusive relationship (referring to her ex-husband) she may have gone too far in the opposite direction herself (meaning from victim to abuser). I began to think my words might have actually done some good. She thanked me for pointing her behavior out to her. However, she said finally, as for me and her, there was no way she could carry on with someone who viewed her in that way - as an abuser. It was just too painful, she said. When I began to reply she hung up on me again!

Now I see that 'closure' was the hook. It wasn't her who wanted closure. She was just annoyed I'd gotten away and wanted to reel me back in again. She was appealing to what she must have figured out was going on inside me. She lured me out of No Contact with the bait of attaining 'closure' and then snatched it away right at the end, leaving things in such a way that it looked as though SHE'D ended it with me (stealing my power of having walked away from HER) and making it seem like she's going to reform, but that I'm the one who's going to miss out.

She SUCCEEDED in making me FEEL (not think - I know in my mind it's all an act) like I might have just let the best thing that ever happened to me slip through my fingers, even though the reality is that this woman is one of the worst things that's ever happened to me (besides the opportunity for personal growth here). I mean, she's really wrecked my heart.

So, it might be old news, but there you are. These kinds of people are deeply deceitful and manipulative. Keep your guard up and don't fall prey to the power of SELF deceit either when it comes time for a hoovering!

Brett's Story

I met a 39yr old single women (or girl as I now believe she is), whilst on tour. We fell quickly. She states she fell before any real contact/conversation other than our eye contact/flirting took place. We had a passionate, physical relationship whilst on a tour together. It felt just amazing, that initial connection.

After 3 weeks, due to prior commitments she returned home, whilst I stayed on tour for a further 3 weeks. At the end of the tour, I went to her country and stayed with her for a week as that was all the time prior commitments for me allowed. It was all such fun, escapism, fantasy, physically the connection was wonderful. Although we speak different languages, everything in my mind seemed fine and the connection seemed very good. We were in love and love was proclaimed on both sides. If apart, we texted and Skyped constantly.

On my second visit, she said noticed a slight change in me. Perhaps, I had brought some stress with me this time (not sure what she saw). She cried like a child due to seeing a small change in me apparently. Her friend told me she overthinks.

Personally, I was so happy and thought there was no need for angst. Within the next week together, after consoling/reassuring her immediately, everything again seemed just beautiful....lots of fun and adoration from both sides. I am very easy-going and saw nothing wrong at all, just perhaps some over-analysis on her part. There seemed no reason to worry.

She cried again as her language lessons had not gone so well. Again, I was there, we talked it through it. She seemed fine, although a little irrational I thought. We were very close. We talked of the future, of me moving in, either in her small flat or maybe renting together. She would not move to my country as this would affect her career and close girlfriend support group. She has therapy every week as part of a support group. She has mother issues as she was controlled as a child.

"Without money there is no love" and "I can live without man, but not without sex." These are two quotes she gave that I clearly remember. She had not had a stable relationship in five years.

She spoke in a child's voice every morning whilst in bed. She liked/loved intercourse, but had trust issues with other areas of our physical relationship.

I went to her country 4 times (4 weeks in total) on holiday for 10 days and she only came to me for a weekend. Was I doing the running? Well, I was going to live in her country, learn the language, so a lot of that made sense to me.

At the airport, she said, "You didn't text much yesterday."

My response was, "We are now away together for 10 days. There is/was no problem."

Eventually, she said, "That was falling in love. We need to find real love."

Push and pull started on her part. She seemed to believe I relied upon her so she woke up occasionally with demons she told me. She also takes sleeping pills and grinds her teeth at night.

"Did the demons involve me?" I would ask.

"No," she would reply. "They are not your concern, though do not be flippant about them. I lose some of you if you are."

I was never angry or flippant...just CONFUSED.

After the holiday, we seemed to have a deeper relationship/closeness. She asked if I would like to move close to her (not in with her), then in her mind her demons may go away over time.

This was not what I wanted to hear. I asked if she loved me. "What is love?" was her reply. She explained that for her love was "trust."

I gave her no reason to mistrust me. I adored her. I was not clingy. In fact, SHE WAS...right up until the day it finished!

Prior to my fourth visit, I began to feel a little insecure. No more girly texts about love and yearnings for a couple of weeks. Ok I thought, let's see how it goes. I arrive. Passion is still there. Fun still there. I meet her parents too...MOM...full of angst. Bang right there, not for me, just full of it.

The demons came back. Ok, let's delve deeper, I thought so I tried to be her therapist. I explained that she had low self-esteem due to past relationships and needed help with her anxiety. She cried, took a deep breath and proclaimed, "I love you. You are a great therapist!" She also was reading a novel "The Red Couch," at the time about therapy.

I looked online about commitment phobia. She went to therapy that evening, apologized on her return for the push and pull/testing stuff on holiday and for 48 hours seemed besotted with me again. I felt odd. Wow, what a turn around, I thought. Yes, she always seemed to adore me physically, but this was like the 'full' return to her former self with me. She was so excited. She didn't want to sleep.

She woke up with demons again the day before I had to leave. In that week, she had also stated she would like me to live with her for 3 months next year as a kind of trial, I guess.

On the last day, she wore my shirt for her day's teaching. She gave me a key to her flat. I told her she was the prettiest teacher in her city. "I hope so," she replied.

Five days later it was over. I finally got a straight answer about her demons because she was to write them down at last. Turns out, she really did not want to tell me because some were about me after all. What a surprise, I thought.

Fear of rejection. Fear of too much love (from me). She was flustered.

She was in control of her emotions and the relationship for the last few weeks. This was clear to me. I, for the first time in months, showed my frustration.

"How can I TRUST you, if you cannot fully explain your demons to me?" I asked. "You told me you loved me a few days ago."

"No, I didn't," she denied. "I also never asked you to move in."

She flat out denied everything she said. I ended the relationship. It was painful, so painful. I neglected to ask so many questions for fear of further hurt.

"How can I tell you I don't know if I love you?" she said. She turned the whole thing around to reject me!! Sad, but true.

Like a little girl, so afraid "FEAR CONQUERED LOVE," she said. She once said, "Maybe you can turn the girl in me to a woman?" She is 39.

Anyway, where did that come from? It was a wet ending to it all.

Every day, she came to ME. She showed me so much affection. SHE, in fact was needy/clingy. Always the last to leave a Skype conversation.

In an email a week later, she wrote me:

"It's' not your fault. I really, really like you. Distance, language, pressure. Your heart was everywhere and nowhere."

Really? I adored everything about her. If I showed too much love she didn't like it. If I wasn't there, she missed me!

Two weeks later out of the blue, she texts and says, "I think of you often and miss many things about you. What are you up to?" Oh yeah, even told me I was her most "potent lover" weeks prior.

The ending was so confusing for me. I obsess daily. Though it is getting easier, I often check websites for analysis purposes (self too) and wonder what it/she was all about. I refuse to respond, hard though as it is.

Andy's Story

I'm new to this forum, but I'm happy I joined because it gave some clarity to some things I'm going through with my girlfriend. When we first met, it was like fireworks. I felt like we were soul mates. She just seemed to love me off the bat and very much wanted me to be in love with her. She seemed like a really great person. When we met, I was in a tight space. I had lost everything - my place and my job. Everything seemed bad at that point, but she didn't seem to care. She still wanted to be with me.

There were times in the course of dating her that she would say off the wall stuff like if she felt someone did something wrong to her, she would set out to get them back in the worst way. Or she would drop off the face of the earth after spending time to get to know a person. She felt those things were funny. I don't know why I didn't see warning signs then. I guess I was just so in love with her.

Anyway, fast forwarding, she asked me to move in with her and she would help me get my life together. I was reluctant at first because I didn't want to ruin our relationship, but I moved in anyway. No sooner than I moved in the house, it just seemed to take the turn for the worse. It felt like we were distant strangers. She wasn't affectionate. She was moody. There were times she would say things like I want my life back, or she would devalue me and treat me like I should put up with her mess since she was paying my way of life. Then in the next breath, she loved me to death and was totally needy.

Her needs came before mine. It was like I had to step on egg shells because I didn't know what would make her crack. Sometimes in the morning, I wouldn't even speak first because I didn't know what mood she was in. Once she would speak, then I would know how to perceive her.

One time I woke up and was excited about a job that I found and I was telling her about it. She cursed me out in an up close and personal outburst. It hurt my feelings and I got quiet. I kid you not, like ten minutes later she was cool and joking with me, like nothing happened. I was speechless as a lot of these things kept happening to the point I was feeling like I was the crazy person. Then there were moments where she just wanted to spend all the time together, and it was no breaks until she said so.

She has done so much, I literally could write a book, but lately she been doing these disappearing acts. Months ago, she basically cut me off and I didn't hear from her for like almost a month in a half. During that time, I was completely heartbroken. I felt abandoned and lost. Mind you now, I have abandonment issues and she was well aware of that, so I blocked her on FB and I didn't call her. I was so love sick to the point I didn't want to live any more. I just didn't understand why she would do that. I was so lost I started calling psychics. I wanted answers that badly. It led to me forming a psychic addiction, which is a hard habit to break.

The break-ups were constant. She would break-up with me and a week later she wanted to be back together. But when she fell off the face of the earth for that month in a half, it really bothered me. She started to try to get in contact with me, but I ignored her because I was so hurt. But after awhile, I decided to talk to her. When she called, she acted as if nothing happened and had the nerve to ask me how long I am going to stay mad at her. I was pissed. I was filled with so much emotion I could scream. I went off on her. Later, I learned that turned her-on because it meant I still loved her!

She asked to be friends and I told her IDK. Then she tried to turn it around by saying, "You don't have to be my friend. That's ok. I shouldn't have asked."

Knowing how I am, she knew I had a weakness for her so she knew after awhile I would give in. Some days had passed and I didn't give in to her wishes so then I get a heap of angry text mgs from her stating I'm broke and calling me a prostitute and everything else. The crazy part at the end of saying all these things, she begged for me to talk to her. I gave in and called her and she was so calm and content.

We got back together. When I took her back everything seemed fine. She would have her occasional outburst, but nothing too extreme. I was so afraid of a repeat of her leaving that I found myself drawing closer to her to the point I abandoned everything in my life. Once I was too dependent, she started claiming I was smothering her and I was controlling. I wasn't any of those things.

It always felt like I was always in the wrong. Sometimes I feel frantic like I did something bad or I did too little or I left her alone too long. I would cancel things with my friends for her. She never put her hands on me, but I still just walked around with that fear of like she did. One time my friend asked me if she was beating me because of how frightened I seemed. Just as soon as she was mean, she would turn around and be nice, better then nice. When that happened, I felt like I was insane because I would get so lost in the good so when the bad happened, I felt like I had been slapped double time.

My worst fears happened again and she did another disappearing act. Mind you now, when she disappeared the last time she was gone for a month and a half and when she returned she boasted about all the things she did (i.e. dates with other women and all kinds of stuff). I finally felt we were better and I fell deeper for her. She made it seem like she was ready to have a family with me and my son.

So here is what happened. She was living with me and for a little bit, things were fine. It finally seemed like we were ok. She just got separated from her husband of 10 years so I know there are some emotions with that. So now she was staying with me. Now her husband had to go to visit his family in another state and she didn't seem to like the idea, even though she didn't want to deal with him at all. I guess it brought back feelings of abandonment so with him leaving she had to move back to her house because her son was there. She moved some of her things out of my house and back to hers and she left a lot of her stuff at my house because she was coming back when her husband returned back to their house. A couple of days passed and she seemed to be getting stranger by the day, but I still spent the night at her house because we were used to sleeping in the same bed together.

My friend came down to stay at my house because her car broke down. We worked at the same place and she needed rides to work. I told my girlfriend about the situation and she acted like everything was fine, and then later on that week she really started to be cold to me. She wouldn't answer my calls, sent short text mgs, and then one day she called me and asked if she could come to my house to get some of her things. I said sure and then I felt a racy feeling like there was something more to the story. Later on that day, when I got home I saw that she took all of her stuff even down to the food she bought when she was living with me. What was the most shocking was she took the bill money that she gave me for bills, which hurt me like a ton of bricks.

I didn't hear from her for close to week and a half. I couldn't even get up the energy to say anything. The strange part is she still was holding on to my key and it scared me a little bit. I didn't know if she was gonna come to my house when I wasn't there. I had no clue. Soon she contacted me and told me she wanted to give my key back. I told her ok, but that I couldn't get it at the minute, but she could drop off the next day. She went crazy saying there is no reason to see me and that she would drop it off at the apt manger. I said fine. The next day, she text me again and asked if I could bring her the external hard drive she left behind. I took it to her house where she gave me back the key without saying a word. My heart sank. I felt like I was nothing anymore. I don't know why I get so emotional when she breaks up with me since she does it all the time. No sooner as I pulled out of the drive way, she calls me to say thank you. I was just like ok and then she calls me again. By this time, I'm enraged.

I answered the phone and I'm like, "What do you want?"

She says, "Do you wanna get something to eat?"

I said fine and circled back to her house to get her. She turns to me and starts acting all jokingly. I just ignored her. She then proceeded to tell me that she was mad because my friend was there and I didn't pay her any attention. I didn't ask her if my friend could stay in my apt so she pegged me as not being loyal. She tried to convince me to kick my friend out and since I didn't, she turned cold again.

Honestly, I felt deep down the end was drawing near. I had a sick feeling like she broke away to engage with another female. Her actions at that time seemed strange and we had stopped being sexual. "Let's take it back a few," she told me. Claimed she didn't have a sex drive, but I found out later it was to control me, and my dumb butt just stayed committed. She started hanging with new people that encouraged her to do bad things. She started to flaunt women in front of me, but she claimed she never cheated on me. They were just friends and they meant nothing. It's just harmful flirting, she would say.

The sex thing really blows me away because one minute she wants it all the time and the next minute, she feels like I disgust her. She accused me of making her my sex slave and said it's all I wanted. It got to the point that I became numb to even asking for anything in that way. Everything was on her terms. Well, she broke up with me again and this time I will be strong and not allow her to come back.

Mike's Story

I was just abruptly discarded after a 1.5 year relationship with my live-in girlfriend who I thought was 'the one.' I'm just over 1 month out and am still in a lot of pain. Recovery has been an excruciatingly slow process. My ex has both narcissism and borderline traits. When I first met her, I tried to take things slow because she was two months out from breaking off an engagement after she discovered her fiancé was cheating on her for the second time.

Her prior long-term relationship also ended because her ex cheated on her. She's a doctor with a demanding schedule, so I excused the cheating as her ex's inability to cope with her schedule. She said they were intimidated by her success. As an attorney, I thought we were a perfect match. This belief was also fueled by what I believe was the idealization stage during which she mirrored my love for sushi, my dog, and passionate sex. I had never been so sure of anything in my life. It was an incredible feeling to be thankful for every decision I had ever made to get me to this point. I was in love.

Over the course of the next few months, I noticed red flags. Turns out she doesn't like sushi, my dog, or sex much. When I confronted her about this, she told me she wasn't comfortable at the beginning of our relationship and now she was. Other red flags included the fact that she talked about money and how much she will make when she is out of residency with increased frequency, how big her engagement ring was, and how she wanted the best life has to offer. I excused a lot of this because she had taken steps to obtain these things. I drove a Porsche, so what is wrong with her wanting a $50k ring? She made the $$ clear.

We had problems with sex from the get go because I didn't feel as though she was enjoying it. It felt very transactional. She'd get mad if I slowed my pace to enjoy the moment. I was under a lot of pressure to finish. Needless to say, this caused some ED problems, which she took personally and would throw in my face. She told me she had never made love with anyone before, that girls don't enjoy sex and only have sex to feel loved. She said she would never allow herself to lose control during sex. She cried a few times during sex as well.

After about 6 months, what I perceived as intimate moments tapered off quite a bit. It got to the point where we only had sex in the mornings because sex at night kept her up. Due to morning breath and her desire to finish quickly, there was no foreplay and we rarely if ever made out. I went into a downward spiral and shifted my focus to work.

We had some really good moments over the next year and some really terrible fights. Most of our fights stemmed from her talking about money, how important her job is and her want for compliments that she claimed I rarely gave. She once said she needed 5 compliments per day.

During our fights, she said the meanest things anyone has ever said to me, things I excused because they were said in the heat of the moment.

Last month, after a few ridiculously busy months at work, she came to me and said she was moving out. The next 7 days were a nightmare of her being hot and cold. She found a place within 3 days and moved out at 6 days. One day, she'd be crying about how she was losing her best friend, and the next day she would be an ice queen. About one week after the move out, she was on an internet dating site telling people she had never been head over heels in love. Reading this was incredibly painful, but I believe it's true, especially if she's a narcissist.

I contacted her about the dating site because she had previously said she had mentioned she would be single for a long time and wanted to respect our relationship. It was a moment of weakness, I know. She responded to say she needed something to distract her from thinking of me, us, and that she was lonely and scared. I took the bait and responded to let her know I miss her so much it hurts. She responded to say she was slammed at work. I went NC and haven't communicated with her since.

Max's Story

When I met my ex, she was in shambles. Her ex-boyfriend had cheated on her and dumped her. I felt sorry for her. I nursed her back and I fell in love with her. We were both in University then. I helped her with her life. I got her out of depression the year after when she could not get a job and supported her. Last year, she wanted to launch her shoe line as she was a podiatrist. I made it a possibility through my connections in the business world. During my University time, I had missed my exams when she was sick to be with her. I did my best to spend time despite my commitments to my law degree and my extracurricular activities. There were a lot of red flags during our relationship, which I ignored because I really loved her. I will make a quick run to the last 4 months of this relationship.

Both of us went overseas and when we got back, I found out she liked somebody else. When I confronted her, she said she cheated on me twice during the relationship, once she had slept with her ex who cheated on her so as to get the control back of her dumping him and not the other way around, and the second time she had cheated with her best friend's cousin. In addition, in the last three months she has been in touch with a guy who she met in a club and she was corresponding to him even during our relationship. She broke up with me, but she kept liking my FB status.

One day, a friend's cousin who is quite attractive came to walk my dog and she made a comment on FB, which I think got her jealous. She lost control and called me from another guy's house and said we should get counselling. I have never been to a psychologist. I agreed to it. Since May, she has mentally abused and psychologically tormented me, blames me for everything that went wrong and tells me I'm not man enough to do a single thing properly. She tells me I am not mature and keeps comparing me to the new guy that she likes. She informs me he is always very attentive to her and listens to her needs, unlike me.

I have done so much for her and splurged a lot of money on her. During the counselling, she accused me and made me feel like a terrible person. The psychologist said it was a toxic relationship and organized for independent sessions. The psychologist also saw through her character and when I confronted my ex about it, she called me a liar. My ex started to blame the psychologist and said the psychologist did not understand her needs.

On the last day of counselling, we had to see the psychologist together. I had decided enough is enough and I said during the session that I did not want to get back together with her. I think my ex was shocked to hear what I said. When we got out of the session, my ex started to cry at the hospital. I felt really bad and even though I wanted to walk away, I could not. I hugged her and said I loved her. Within a few moments, she started to talk about this guy and how great he is. I felt like a knife stuck through my heart and I fell for her trap again.

She seemed to be having fun, going out for movies and having the time of her life as she lied to our common friends that I had moved on and was dating other girls, which was not true. I fell into depression and suffered terribly from it. During those months, I tried calling her and speaking to her, not understanding what went wrong in my life. I really missed her. She abused me and threatened me that she was going to get a restraining order against me, but all I wanted was to get closure from her. I called her maybe only once a week. She had changed her number twice on me and I decided enough was enough so I started to move ahead with my life. I was still involved through the business relationship I helped to create for her, but I remained aloof during the whole time.

Three weeks ago when I spoke to her, she said she loves this guy and she thinks he is the one and she is going to get married to him. I said fine and congrats. Two weeks ago, we had to catch up for a conference call and I spoke strictly business with her. I left the conversation after which there had been emails from her, which I replied directly and to the point.

In the last week, her relationship with her business partner, who was a contact through my contact, fell apart. I got 4 calls from unknown numbers on my mobile phone and a voice mail from my ex telling me that she would call back. I got a call again that evening from her and told her I was busy and would speak to her later. Again on Monday, I got 5 calls this time with exposed numbers. It was her and she had also sent me an email saying she called. She called me again on Tuesday and I spoke to her.

She blamed me that it was my fault her business fell through and that she could have done it all by herself. She told me that she is entirely capable of pulling it through by herself. I asked her why she was calling me and telling me this and she said "We were in a relationship together for 3 and a half years and that I was a great guy with a good heart and she would like to be friends." She kept whining about what had happened. I listened to her and I showed sympathy to her. She said she would like to be invited to things that I attend. I said we shall see. I kinda think I fell for her words, which happens every time she speaks to me.

She said we don't have a future and I never asked her for a second chance and she abused me calling me names. I asked her where she is staying and she said she is still staying at this guy's house. I recalled what she said 2 weeks ago to me. I asked her if he is so good to her, why they're not getting married. She told me she is too young. I asked her if she is still going out with him and she said no, but that she needs to be with him, which I totally did not understand what she meant by that. Before we finished the conversation, she said to me, "Now that you have my number, do not call me every day or else I will change the number."

I was totally struck by what this meant because I never called her in the last 3 weeks. In fact, she was the one calling me over 12 times in the last week. I immediately deleted her new number from my phone after the call.

Melanie's Story

My story is the same as everyone's.....filled with pain, anger, self-doubt and fear. The only difference is we were a lesbian couple married for two years. I have joined this forum not knowing if she truly has NPD or if I am just trying to make sense of a senseless situation.

We met 5 years ago and omg it was crazy. We were so much in love. She kept saying that it was sad because everyone else only thought they were in love-only we knew the real thing! I was successful, had a good career, home and was more than comfortable money wise. She was a receptionist at a low budget hotel, living in one room. We spent every moment together and felt that life was simply perfect. She told me about her previous relationships, how she had only ever had "crazy" women until now of course.

After a short whirlwind romance, my job became insecure and we needed to make some big decisions. Crazy but without a thought, we put what we could in the back of the car and moved to France. All the possessions I had worked so hard for, sold or given away. This is when the cracks started to show. She began over-reacting to the smallest situation. Being left waiting would bring about irrational and noisy protests. Driving in the car was always stressful and occasionally downright dangerous. I recall one occasion where she tried to run a cyclist off the road because he had not let her pass. To this day, she believes he deserved it! This is also when I saw how mean she could be to others - particularly her family. But none of this mattered because I thought she would never treat me that way. We were perfect and the happiest day of my life was the day we married.

Time passed and things were good. We moved back to the U.K. but slowly something changed. I became frustrated at her moodiness, which she said was my fault. I was tired of her laziness with household chores and concerned by her deep-seated belief that rules, laws and socially accepted behavior did not apply to her if it didn't meet her needs. But I still believed she was my perfect wife. I bought her expensive presents, tended to her every wish and took her on exotic holidays. I would have done anything for her. But things soon turned sour - she started wearing sexy underwear for work, much more make-up than I had ever seen her wear. She changed passwords and became secretive with her phone. I knew the signs, but when challenged she would freak out. Call me a jealous suspicious cow with trust issues. We split up for a couple of months with her telling everyone she could no longer deal with my crazy behavior!

Convincing me she was right, I went back to her promising I would change. After all, it was just me being crazy, right? For a week or so everything seemed perfect. I ignored the fact that she was having private calls and sneaking off to see friends without me. We even made plans for our much longed-for baby. Everything was going to be fine. Then the night before she was due at the baby clinic, she told me she missed her friends and was moving to be closer to them - 300 miles away from me!

She said she loved me, but wasn't happy. That was when I found the love letters from her girlfriend. All the same expressions she had used on me. How perfect they are together and how she wished everyone could be as happy as them. So now, she is gone. I made her leave straight away after an extremely violent outburst when I confronted her with the letter. Apparently, my finding out was justification for this. What did I expect??

I've been sleepless and checking my phone every 30 seconds, hoping for contact, hoping for the woman I still love (?) to be out there trying to find her way home. I loathe myself for being so pathetic. Where is my self-respect? I know I am so much better off without her and am not even sure what she brought to the relationship (apart from great sex of course), but I miss her and want the pain to stop.

Don's Story

This is my story. About 10 years ago, I met someone from where I live who I thought was the answer to all my prayers and dreams. I was a single father, raising 2 small boys at the time and this lady was all I had ever dreamed of. She was fun to be around, loved life as much as I did, was great with my boys, and was a great homemaker...anything and everything a guy could ask for.

For the first 3 years we were together, I was the soul breadwinner. I worked and she stayed home and took care of the kids and house. After that, she got the itch for a job and a car so we went and got a car. I cosigned for it and she got a job to pay the note on it and everything was pretty normal so far, right?

Well, the boys wanted to go live with their mother and I didn't want to deprive them of that experience. Shortly after that is when trouble started. I no longer was receiving child support so money was tight. Her mother, so she said, was having problems at home, and she thought it would be best if she moved back home and helped her. I didn't think anything of it because if it was my mom, I would have done same thing.

Three weeks after she moved, I called to see if she wanted to get together that weekend. Her mother's boyfriend answered the phone and said she wasn't there and wouldn't be back until middle of the following week. I was like, huh what??? I must mention I live in Tennessee. She took off to look for a job in New Mexico with no word to me, no notice, nothing.

Well, she got the job and moved out there. I find out she traced down an ex-husband who is a scientist out there and went to be with a man she hadn't gotten over so to speak. Well, he was married and she played second fiddle for 18 months and then moved back home because she wanted to see me. She said that maybe, just maybe, we could hang out, be friends and see what develops.

I was so excited to be given the chance to at least try and work things out. For six months, I tried and she kept telling me she was happy with the way things were for the moment with us. She moves 2 hours away with no warning, no notice, no nothing. I decided I am so done and over all of this crap. I will take the $7,500.00 loss that she left me with, move on and find someone else.

I did find someone else, nothing alike but all I REALLY needed in my life. She loved me for who I was, not what I had or could give her. We got engaged and were fixing to be married in the fall. I was over the narc and was moving on with my life. I was really happy.

Then 2 weeks before the end of last year, I get an email from the ex narc with photos of us when we were together - all the great times and happy times we spent together talking about how we really were a great couple. She wished me luck on my forthcoming marriage, but said it eventually wouldn't work out. I freaked out. She wanted to see me and talk about old times and just hang out.

I took the bait. I went to see her two hours away, spent the entire night listening to her tell me how sorry she was, how she made a mistake and that I was right when I said karma would catch up to her. It did pretty badly. I ended staying there for 2 days. All she wanted to do was tell me how sorry she was and to please forgive her and let's try again. For 2 days that's the way it was. I'm thinking, yeah she's learned her lesson and has really changed this time.

I broke the relationship off with my fiancé. I broke her heart and in the long run, mine as well. I never should have betrayed her because nine months later, I was told by the narc that she had made a mistake 9 months ago since having sex with me. She found me sexually unattractive and all she wanted was to be friends now.

I am 50 years old and have never been told this. Let me say, during the first couple months we were back together, I was receiving insurance checks from my mother's passing and she was in a tight financial spot due to not working and behind on rent and car problems, etc. Being so in love with her, I took all that money and got her rent caught up and got her car fixed. Too many things to mention here that I took care of for her. Then after all of this, I am now not worthy enough to sleep with and be with all of the time. Now, only when it was convenient for her, a total of 8 years I was with her and 10,000.00 dollars in debt, I ended up filing bankruptcy because of it all.

One month after what I assumed were final words with her, I get a call from her after my father passed away wondering if there was anything she could do and that she was sorry about my dad. I told her yeah there was ....to continue her quest in finding someone more sexually attractive and with a larger bank account and to please leave me alone because I could no longer handle her narcissistic sociopathic ways.

She asked me not to put her down because she was only trying to be nice and help during the loss of my father one week after he was dead and buried. She's gonna try and help, yeah ok. Well, now she's rubbing her new romance in my face. She has found someone who makes 3 times more money than me.

She's so happy with her new life. I, on the other hand, have felt like I'm spiraling out of control from all the hurt and emotional anguish. Everything I did, I did out of love for her and only wanted what I thought to be best. I haven't heard from her since I told her not to bother me anymore, but the last thing I said was once you've punched your ticket on the karma express it will come into your station a lot harder and faster than before and all she could say was, "Oh well, guess if it happens, it happens."

So here's the thing, narcs follow a cycle and this looks like a narc cycle to me. After all the fun and games of her new life wear thin, am I going to have to deal with this again?

Kevin's Story

Needless to say, I never in a million years thought I would end up in a support group like this. The term NPD was never something I had ever heard of until a few months ago. Maybe it's society's expectation of men, pride, ego, or a combination of all of the above, but I am so angry with myself, embarrassed, and humiliated with myself. It's ridiculous. No one I know seems to understand what I'm dealing with. After a few weeks of research, I decided to post here as a means of healing and support.

I met who I believed was my perfect match. My 10 year marriage had ended 3 years prior, and I purposely took my time to heal and work through my part of my failed marriage. It was a long and difficult journey examining my life, my shortcomings, and my core beliefs to get to a place where I truly felt ready to love someone. I read everything I could about love, went through extensive therapy, and belonged to several church groups. In the end, what I desired to be was someone who aspired to love the way God had instructed in 1 Corinthians 13. We all know it: "love is patient, love is kind" and so on.

When I met her she presented herself as everything I ever wanted. She told me she was divorced after an 18 year marriage to a much older man. It was his 2nd marriage and they had two children together who were teenagers. She was on the board of several local charities and talked about how important having a sense of community was to her. I admired her spirit, her loyalty, her commitment to her children and how kind she appeared to be.

Like many of the stories I've read, it wasn't long before I noticed some inconsistencies. She in fact, was not yet divorced, but rather going through a very acrimonious property settlement with her estranged husband. She told she was 46, when in fact she was 49. She told me she was divorcing him, when in fact he had moved out and filed for divorce a year prior. All huge red flags for me, but I chose to stay the course, believing part of love means believing the best in people.

We talked for hours about doing things the right way this time, about communicating to each other our hopes, fears, insecurities, and triumphs. I was completely hooked. We dated for a few months before having the talk about being exclusive. I had no desire to date anyone but her, and she concurred even though her divorce was not yet final.

Things for the next 7 or 9 months were absolutely lovely, or so I thought. She talked incessantly about her divorce, his 5 adult kids from his first marriage, all she sacrificed for him and how he owed her. She played the victim to the hilt and I fell head first into wanting to protect and support her.

After the divorce was finalized, I foolishly thought things would continue to improve between us and our relationship would begin to transition into a more traditional one. She lied pathologically to virtually everyone. Whatever would give her the most sympathy was the story she would tell. Her son had broken his back and she told me it happened when he was with his dad during summer vacation. Two weeks later, she told some acquaintances it happened during football. Another time, she told her friends it was a genetic disorder because he grew 6 inches in a year.

On another occasion, she told me she was attending a cancer charity event where they were going to honor her friend and next door neighbor who was a supporter of the cause. She said her neighbor's husband had purchased several tables for his late wife's friends as a way to honor her legacy. Several days later, her photograph from the event is in the society section with her arm around another man. I point-blank ask her if she was on a date and she denied it saying they just grouped a bunch of people together to take the photo and that she didn't even know the man.

A few days later, she says it was a co-worker of her friend's husband. A month later, I'm at her house and the phone rings at 11:30 p.m. and the caller-id pops up with this guy's name. She tells me his son died and she was just supporting him - how dare I be so selfish (a ploy she knows will get me). I ask her why she didn't just tell me the truth and she tells me it's because she never had a relationship where she could just be honest about something like that.

Now I consider myself a very reasonable guy so I told her to just tell me the truth. I can handle it. I told her if she wanted to date other people to just let me know so I can base my future on the facts. She reassures me that I am the only one and she is sorry that she lied.

Several months later, my friend sees her profile on a dating website and forwards the link to me via email. When confronted, she goes ballistic accusing me of spying on her and telling me I'm the most insecure man she has ever met. She tells me it's my fault that I don't have a full and satisfying life and I need to put all my energy into her and what she is doing.

All the intimate details of my life that I shared with her are now being thrown in my face as a means to hurt me. My parents are both deceased, along with my brother. She tells me she wants to be with someone who has a family. I swear I felt like I was losing my freaking mind. I felt minimized at every turn. When I tried to talk to her about how I felt she says her life is extremely hectic with selling her house and dealing with her son's back. She tells me she just doesn't have time to cater to my needs.

Note....total projection!

There are countless stories like this with her. I end the relationship and inevitably she comes back days or weeks later saying she is sorry that she hurt me. She promises that it won't happen again, etc. Like a fool I want to believe her and believe that love will never fail if I do it the way God instructed, but my soul is screaming at me - Don't Do It!

Finally a month ago, a friend from my "small world" (that's how she refers to my life) calls me and says they are working on a charity committee with my girlfriend. They tell me the president of the charity, who they are both friends with, says my girlfriend goes on more dates than anyone she knows but none of them are boyfriends - wow.

Mind you, earlier that day she tells me how she can't wait to marry me and spend every day with me. In the same breath, she says she hates that her kids ask about me. I kid you not, 15 minutes later, another friend sends me her profile from Match.com.

That was 1 month to the day I have blocked her from calling me, emailing me and every other means of communication. I now realize that none of it was real. She is a very sick woman who will never get better. I've had numerous relationships, but nothing that even remotely resembles this. I feel foolish, humiliated, and deceived. The worst part is that I know I could have stopped it early on before it got to this point. I feel as if I'm in a fog and have been for quite some time. It's hard to focus on anything other than this, but I realize that I must accept some of the responsibility for choosing to stay in this unhealthy relationship. My focus will now be on me. What do I need to change internally so that I don't settle for this type of behavior again? I know who I am, what I have to give, and my ability to love.

Shawn's Story

I'm sorry this is long but I'm so hurt and want people to know that men too get hurt and taken advantage of by women. I met this professional woman online and during the first month I didn't ask her to be in a relationship with me. She liked me as well during that time, but she didn't pursue me either. We spent some weekends together, but never actually became an exclusive couple. We eventually went our separate ways and dated others.

Months later, I came back into her life and we started going out. She said she had been seeing a guy for two months, but said she loved me and had always loved me. Eventually, she asked this other guy for her house key back and told him she wanted to see other people. This was right after she and I went to Philly together for 5 days. However, according to her she did not tell him specifically that the reason for the breakup was me. She had always said that she had never left one man for another man and she didn't want to start now. So she never actually stopped seeing this other guy and she continued to see me as well.

Over the next three months, she and I traveled extensively taking trips out of state, hotels, bed and breakfasts, Eastern Shore, D.C. on the 4th of July, Atlantic City, etc. We had the BEST time every time. She was mostly honest with me about still seeing this other guy, which I hated knowing but I accepted.

Anyway, during these months, she spent more time with me than him, but it still bothered me that she wouldn't commit to me. She always lied to him when she was with me. As hurtful as it is to admit, she would always post our trips on her Facebook page, but I was never tagged or even shown in the photos. Her photos consisted of things such as the hotel we were at, sunsets, restaurants, shows we attended, a landmark, the food/wineglasses at our table, etc. but never once was I shown on FB with her. I have many photos of us together on these vacations, but out of respect I didn't post them on FB either. I let her control the situation.

She said she was just trying to spare his feelings and I accepted it because I was hoping that I would eventually be with her forever. That was probably one of the most hurtful aspects of this relationship. Knowing I was being hidden away like she was cheating on a husband or boyfriend. She said she was very confused and often questioned why I didn't grab her back in February when I had the chance.

When she went out with him, on the other hand, she would post it on Facebook and also tag him. It made me feel awful to know she would do that with him but not me. She claimed it was because people assumed they were still dating. She would also disappear for days and not respond to texts or voice mails I left. Once in a while, I'd get a text that said, "I love you more than you know." That's it. Then I'd be ignored again while she's out having a good time and rubbing my nose in it on Facebook, which was extremely hurtful as well. She always managed to call me days later like everything was okay and always had some kind of excuse.

This woman initially bombarded me with words that made me feel awesome. She said she loved this other guy too, but her love for me was different - with me she had such passion. She was IN love with me versus just loving the other guy. She built me up. She said if the other guy left or dated someone else, it wouldn't be a huge deal, but if I were to leave or date someone else, it would destroy her. She made me feel so special and she was so much fun. I found her to the most beautiful woman in the world. Not a woman alive could make me feel as special as she did. There's no question I would be there for her forever. Looking back though, I feel I was more addicted to this woman than in love with her.

Anyway, there was always so much drama, which went on for months. It took its toll on me. I lost over 40 lbs. going from 211 down to a low of 169. I don't know why I couldn't just leave. It was like she literally had a spell on me.

So about a month ago, I take her out to eat. We have drinks and we're having a great time. We go back to her place and it's around midnight...still having a great time. We're having some wine, eating some food in bed and barely dressed. It's literally the best time of my life, to be honest, and then there's a bang on the door. It's him. He yelled inside that he knew I was there (my car was out front). I knew she wouldn't just allow him to stand outside and bang on the door so I opened the door. To make a long story short, she asked ME to leave and he stayed!

I was completely disgusted and totally devastated. He basically just took my spot in bed. I was totally numb and in a fog. This girl said I meant so much to her. She unfriended me on all social media sites and never called me again.

I tried contacting her and was successful sometimes. She said that she unfriended me on all social media sites because she doesn't want to hurt me any more by seeing pictures of him and her together. There's no remorse though at all. She said she's going to try to work it out with this guy.

My entire life has been affected. I go to sleep thinking of her. I dream about her. I wake up in the middle of the night thinking of her. Why do I feel like this after being treated like this? Seems I should consider myself lucky that she went with this guy and left me alone, but does anyone think she will leave me alone forever? It's almost like I WANT her to come back. How sick am I??

I kind of figured maybe I was the transitional victim of a sociopath. Sociopaths use people to satisfy their temporary needs in between long term victims. She always said she loved me, but she never actually demonstrated her love to me. Aside from a few dinners at the beginning, she never spent a dime on me. She also never showed remorse or guilt about anything that happened between us. I often wonder if she simply tried to destroy me emotionally for fun.

I used to be a healthy guy, but now I'm in therapy, on sleep medication, anxiety medication and something else prescribed to calm my nerves. I'm still a freaking mess. The last time I spoke with her she said she loved me and would always love me. BTW, she just got engaged to this guy and they're getting married next month. It's so crazy.

Doug's Story

Seven months on, still dealing with it. It has been seven months since the breakup, and almost three months since I had a text convo with her. I still feel the pain, but more and more I am accepting what she is/was. My mind for a long time has fought between what was real and what was an illusion. And it has been torture. So odd how over time, your mind only sees and believes what it wants. Disconnection or rather the life of living in an illusion and forcing your gut and heart to believe in "ignorance is bliss."

So many realizations have popped into my memories. When we first dated, I remember her telling me so many things that should have been red flags, but I thought nothing about them.

- When she talked about the songs she loved, such as Cindy Lauper's "Time After Time," she explained that the song was about how you never know when the person you love might be gone with the blink of an eye and with no explanation. She then said, "Watch out."
- Other songs she loved were songs about a cheating lover. The song, "Someone that I Used to Know" was one of her favorites.
- The dream she had about me cheating on her with someone I never met and then telling me that she loves me and that she will just have to accept it when it happens is total projection, I believe.
- Her ex constantly texted her because he was confused about what happened, and how much pain he was in. He knew nothing about me.
- All the triangulation. Either about ex men or her friends and family, none of which was true but I believed.

She told me she cheated once in her life on her ex before me. I later found out she cheated on every man she had ever been with and left them all for no real reason, other than that she no longer felt excitement any more.

Her other term was "I no longer feel for someone, and then I leave for a new person." None of her ex men where abusive, but she would go back and forth telling me they were. She always played the victim at first.

She controlled how I acted. Controlled when we met, and if anything was not how she wanted, she punished me. I saw all of these signs and yet grew very accustomed to it over time, just saying to myself, "It's just what she wants and how she is....I want to keep her happy."

So many things I saw and heard, and that she actually told me. I thought that I was different and that as long as I gave her what she wanted/needed, we would be ok. But that was her "conditioning" me to allow and accept her treatment because "our love" and relationship was different. It was a trap so I could give her an attractive, successful, and caring man as a slave and emotional play toy. I knew deep down that eventually I would be discarded, but my stupid heart didn't want to believe it.

She suddenly left after expressing how happy she was with me on a daily basis, and how thankful she was to have me in her life. She immediately jumped to her next victim - an older and bald man from her work. She is 28 he is 40 year old. I see him as a good source because I don't think an older unattractive man would put his foot down too much being with an extremely very beautiful younger woman.

At first, she seems so sweet, innocent and perfect. Sex is her tool she uses, and a very innocent, victimized, caring personality is her trap.

No Contact works fellas. I believe she is BPD/NPD, but also psychopathic. Please for your own life... run when you first get funny feelings or see flags. You can't beat these people. They are master manipulators and will get to you the longer you are with them. They don't just attack your pride. They attack everything you are, both mentally and emotionally. Once you see that, it is way too late.

Jason's Story

Controlling or an N? I'll put the issues in point form for an easier read.

She:

- Appears sweet and funny
- Has friends who love her
- Is very independent and seems to care for her friends and family
- Does volunteer work (hardly seems narcissistic)
- Joked early on that she 'baited and switched' in relationships (As in, she started off sweet, 'baited' guys and then 'switched' to what she was really like)
- Became instant Facebook friends with my mother after meeting her for the first time
- Told me she had 'emotional walls'
- Told me her previous boyfriend had told her she had a temper, but he was boring and she dumped him and never looked back
- Had to bring her own muesli (in a sealed bag), her own tea bags, blankets and pillows when she stayed at my place because she could not eat or drink anything else for breakfast
- Had a rule that no blanket sharing and no touching was allowed after sex

She didn't talk to me for 3 days after her friend's wedding. She wouldn't answer my calls except once, where she said, "You don't want to know what I've got to say to you" and then hung up. Three days later, she finally called. By the way, at this wedding, I didn't know anyone there and she was a bridesmaid so lots of sitting on my own trying to make conversation. Anyway when she called she had a list of things I'd done wrong. She accused me of being drunk (which I was not), not talking to her enough, not saying goodnight (which admittedly I didn't do when we got home because I fell asleep) and 'pushing her onto the bed, which

I did do but not in an aggressive way, but in a passionate way as we were kissing. I would NEVER EVER hurt anyone physically. I apologized and felt so awful and agreed to stop drinking, although I am not a big drinker.

She then thought "I was wonderful" and she went back to being happy, delightful and funny. During this conversation I even said, "Look, if this is too hard for you or you think we're too different, let's end it."

She said, "No no. It's because I care about the relationship that I want these things to stop. If I didn't care, I'd just break up with you."

I also had to buy a separate wedding present from hers as she had already bought one, which was from 'her' not 'us' and I had only met this friend once.

But soon it continued.

- She had a temper tantrum when I had the music up too loud. She locked herself in her room. I apologized and agreed that the music was too loud.
- Told me I was very sensitive. I agreed that I could be, but suggested that sometimes she could be moody too. She abruptly told me, "No, I'm not" in a very aggressive, end-of-conversation way.
- Told me that she couldn't possibly watch me play guitar because she would be "too embarrassed."
- Told me that I was one of those "emotional guys."
- Told me that she had dated a guy who played the guitar like me and it was awful. "Too emotional. It was terrible," she said.
- Couldn't say "I love you" if I had said it as she didn't want to feel like she had to because I had. She preferred to say "ditto."

- Told me that she had better things to do and would have preferred to be somewhere else after watching me play soccer once.

- Told me in her previous relationship she had done too many things she didn't want to do and was determined that wasn't going to happen again.

- Told me she could not visit my family because I had a cigarette 3 months ago and that had broken her trust. If I even had so much of a drag of a cigarette in the future, she would break up with me and that it would be my fault.

- Didn't want any alcohol in her life (with no explanation), and then wanted to know how many drinks I would be having at my best mate's wedding, where I was the best man. I had to tell her exactly how many drinks I would be having or she wouldn't come.

- She seemed to be so nice to her friends. I don't even think they'd believe me if I told them what she could be like with me behind closed doors.

- Threatened to leave one night if I watched 30 minutes of sport. I had not watched any sport with her for 7 months.

- Told me I was not very creative, which was disappointing.

- Got angry if I left my keys on her desk. Got angry if I left my toiletries bag in the bathroom.

- Got angry when I suggested a movie that wasn't a girl's film. I think it was Robin Hood.

- Got angry when I didn't text her back in the appropriate time.

- Got angry when I didn't text her enough when I was overseas for 2 weeks so we had to speak on the phone every night.

- Asked me to move in with her, but it had to be in her chosen suburb with none of my old furniture and it had to happen on a particular month.

- No chocolate would be allowed in the house.

- She chose clothes for me that were "cooler" than what I was wearing.
- Was obsessed with exercise and looked down on people (like me) who like to have a drink sometimes.
- Told me I watched too much TV. I work in TV so sometimes I watch it.
- She once told me in the car that she thought we should have a fight for no reason.
- She once told me she wanted to hit me but for no reason.
- She didn't like my taste in music and made me feel foolish because of it.
- She only seemed happy when we were doing exactly what she wanted to do. Everything else was a chore.
- She made me feel guilty over things I liked, like somehow they were dumb or boring.
- I had to agree with her or the consequences were anger or critical dismissal.

She got angry when I kissed an old friend on the lips (who is married with 2 kids with her husband standing there). I agreed to simply kiss her on the cheek in future as I didn't want her to feel uncomfortable. That was no good. I had to tell her I would never see her again. I disagreed, as I had tried to compromise. Her compromise was to not see me if I saw this friend. She was very angry with me for the next 2 nights.

During that week she then told me she was going away for 3 days because she was angry with me. I told her that I'd like to come so we could work on things rather than silence for 3 days. She agreed, and later was all smiles and enthusiasm again. I met loads of her friends and did what she wanted to do, but by the last day she changed. She wouldn't let me kiss her or hold hands. She had turned into a different person.

In the car ride home she said, "Next time, I'm coming on my own. I felt suffocated with you here. I have not enjoyed the weekend because of you and I was so embarrassed when you read the paper." I briefly read the paper in the afternoon.

At the time, I had never felt so insulted and hurt by someone that was supposed to love me. I have never seen such disregard for someone else's feelings, efforts and compromise. It was like a switch in her head had changed and now she saw me as pathetic. She made me feel as if I was at fault for her feeling the way she did.

How do you come back from that? How do you have any self-respect left? After all the compromise, doing what she wanted to do over the past 7 months, my apologies for not living up to her expectations, the guilt, being made to feel inadequate, she never once appreciated my good qualities, but focused only on the bad.

I told her in the car that I didn't want to see her any more. She angrily responded, "Fine" and dropped me in the rain and left me to get a train home.

The next day, I told her that I was sorry that it had to end and that perhaps I was just too sensitive (self-blame) to continue the relationship. I told her she had fantastic qualities, friends and family and I would miss her.

She replied, "I'm relieved it's over. I constantly had to compromise my happiness to make you happy. We could never talk about our problems (clearly not true as you have seen above). Goodbye."

She never contacted me again, never showed any remorse and blamed the downfall of the relationship on me.

I loved her...head over heels love. I didn't see red flags. I didn't see the subtle put downs. I didn't see that very slowly she was trying to control me by making me feel bad. She didn't do it much in the beginning and her occasional temper outburst was always quickly hidden. It was all excitement and enthusiasm. It was like she was waiting for me to fall for her and then she could start molding me into what she wanted, which is exactly what happened.

With someone who has such self-belief, confidence and a clear idea of her ideal world, it's hard to disagree so I turned her criticisms back on myself. I believed them. Suddenly I didn't know what to say, what to do, or what to like. I also tried harder to make myself better than in any other relationship ever. I don't understand how someone can be so enthusiastic, so joyful, so excited by us and then turn around every three weeks and make you feel bad about yourself.

She told me her parents "truly hated each other" but stayed together because her mom was Catholic. Surely growing up with that must affect someone. Both parents were totally devoted to her and I think she got away with whatever she wanted.

It was only 7 months, that was 6 months ago and I still think about what I should've done better. If only I didn't do that or liked what she liked more. Surely this was true love is what I've been thinking. How else do I explain my certainty that she was the one and all the excitement and nerves? I wanted to be a better man for her, but it seemed like being a better man was to be more like her version of a better man.

Now she has proudly displayed her new boyfriend and her as her FB profile. I know about NC. It was dumb. I shouldn't have done that. It's brought it all back because I'm now thinking, 'Well, it must have been me. Look how happy she is. She's finally met the right guy and he's getting all her wonderful qualities and not the bad ones. What a lucky guy. If only I could have been more of what she wanted, I'd have that.'

I have never had such a problem getting over someone. The highs were so high it must have been love, right? I've come out of it thinking she's absolutely convinced that it was my fault and she did nothing wrong. Why can't I think differently? Why am I going through this awful process of self-blame and regret?

One minute, she thought I was great and the next minute, nothing but anger and disapproval. It doesn't make sense and the only way I've been able to make sense of it is blaming myself. Surely it's my fault that this girl who is loved by friends and family was angry/disappointed with me? I don't think I've met anyone like her. When it was good, it was the best. It was so exciting, funny and passionate. Clearly I wasn't enough.

Ray's Story

Spinning in Circles. Exactly one month ago, I ended a relationship with what I thought was the love of my life when I discovered all the lies deceit and betrayal that had been occurring since day one of our relationship.

I'm a guy in my early to mid-twenties, just getting started in my career after finishing up a degree. I've only ever had 2 serious relationships. Preparation for my career has always been first and foremost in my life. The first ended when she and I realized that our lives were just not on the same page. After some initial bitterness, things calmed down and we are on friendly terms. The last serious relationship ended with lies, cheating and betrayal on her part, and after much honest evaluation, looking back, and reading, it's clear she fits the example of a narc.

Knowing is one thing, adjusting, another completely. It's like my heart hasn't caught up with my head in the logic department. I've decided to post here because I just need to let it out, be heard and maybe even get some advice, because quite honestly, I can't shake this funk that I am in.

In my line of work, I've seen some pretty horrible things. I've had to do things that people who aren't in this line of work would never understand. That's not a bad thing as it's taught me to maintain composure and control my emotions in even the worst situations. Don't get me wrong, I don't repress emotion and bad feelings. It's just an unspoken rule, you don't talk about it. You internally sit down, analyze and adapt, eventually moving on.

I realize it's only been a month, but I haven't made any progress at all. It feels like for every step forward, I take two back. I've tried talking to friends, but that's just not cutting it. I am not accustomed to sharing my thoughts and feelings with others and it's uncomfortable. They sympathize and are trying to help, but they just don't get it. Every single one of my friends is in a solid happy long term relationship. It's hard just being around them and seeing the happiness I thought I had, but ultimately discovered was just an act.

Now for the relationship, the whole thing started with a lie. She was with another guy when we first started talking. When I found out I immediately backed off. She and all her friends assured me that this guy was not with her. He was just a jealous stalker type that always wanted to be with her, but she was never interested. My intuition was that this wasn't true, but I ignored it and continued to pursue the relationship....my first mistake.

Things progressed over time and we decided to be exclusive, eventually turning into her telling me she "loved" me. She remained in contact with some of her ex's but always made it a point to tell me when she spoke with them so that I would know I could trust her and that there was nothing there. What I found out later was that she was actually keeping avenues open so she could go back if things weren't working out between us.

At first, I felt like I'd never felt in a relationship before. She made me feel like I was the center of her world. Affection everywhere, close was never close enough, she challenged me to be a better boyfriend- open up, express myself, etc.

As the relationship progressed, we eventually got to the point where we both found ourselves in new jobs; mine was the first real opportunity I had at making a career, not just a stepping stone to something greater. There was a lot of stress adjusting to these changes, especially because it was extremely close to the holidays. I had to adjust my sleep schedule and behaviors to adapt to my new work environment and this caused a conflict in the sense that I had to allow extra time for me to make sure I could adjust and perform at my best because like I said, people rely on me to keep them safe and my partners have to count on me to protect them as well.

Man oh man, did things change once my focus drifted even the tiniest bit away from her. Up until this point, I would bend over backwards to keep her happy, do things I didn't want to do, even give up some of my passions to keep her happy because she didn't like that it interfered with our time together.

I got out of shape, alienated friends for her just because they happened to be female even though the relationship with them was completely platonic. We had known each other since we were 10 years old for crying out loud! I thought I was happy because making her happy was what made me happy. Looking back, I now realize that it was so draining, and I was blinded by how she made me feel at the beginning. I held on to that feeling, even though I knew it had been slipping away more and more.

About the beginning of December, the changes in the relationship had become so apparent, so numerous, and so intense that I couldn't attribute it to just stress and change anymore. I confronted her about this growing distance between us, the lack of affection and intimacy on her part, her care free attitude about being with her new friends, mostly guys, out late, not knowing where she is or who she is with (mind you it was a big deal if I got a text from a female friend asking for help with something work related, but her behavior was to be considered ok), but she was not willing to do anything to spend any time with me. Her answer was that she was unhappy because I am never conversational, I don't show her I love her and I'm always sleeping (I start my 13 hour shifts at 4am), etc.

Now, I am the first to admit my faults. I am not afraid of criticism, and as I loved this girl, I was more than willing to listen. I know I am not very conversational. She would ask me about work and I would be very short and non-descriptive, such as "Oh you know, long day, really busy" and not much else. Not because I didn't want to share, but because of the nature of my job, it would be a crime to share. She knew this and I stretched the rules to their very limit, but I'm not a big small talker either and I told her that I will definitely make the effort to be more involved in the conversations and not just listen to her.

The sleeping, I tried to explain. I need to be able to perform my job to the best of my abilities for the safety of myself and others, but I conceded that I could push my sleep schedule a little more when I had days off and promised I would.

115

The affection and intimacy, or lack-of, she blamed on me because my actions had put her in a bad mood. I attributed not showing I loved her to my lack of experience in serious relationships. She cried a lot, but ultimately at the end, I felt like it was all my fault, that I had failed her in some way by making her upset.

The next few days were rocky. She was extremely cold and I was trying to maintain an 'it's ok, we will get through this and be stronger for it' positive attitude for her so she wouldn't be upset.

Then I got our cell phone bill the day after Christmas. I noticed an extremely high volume of calls from her line-almost 1000 minutes on her line alone. I looked at the detailed usage and discovered she would spend anywhere between an hour and a half to three hours on the phone at 2-3 in the morning with this number. I looked into it and found out it was a guy she worked with. This had been going on for several weeks, about the time I noticed this distance starting to manifest itself.

I confronted her immediately, as I was at work we discussed it on the phone. I stepped away from where I had the bill open on the computer and we talked on and off for almost 7 hours. Finally, it felt as if a giant weight had lifted off my chest. I thought I finally got through to her. She apologized and assured me it was nothing more than her venting her frustrations about the issues we were having with another guy so he could give her insight her girlfriends couldn't. I bought into it, that is until I sat back down and looked at the computer. The bill had refreshed since I last looked at it. Every time I had to let her go, or she had to let me go, she was on the phone with this guy (we will call him John from now on).

She called again to tell me she missed me and would really like it if I would just go to her place and curl up and watch a movie. Knowing full well what she had been doing I agreed, like I had no idea and everything was ok. I was not going to deal with any more lies on the phone. I'd see if she would lie to my face. I needed to actually do my job anyways, luckily it was a quiet day and the distraction wasn't really harmful.

The work day ended and I just went straight to her house. I didn't shower, didn't change, and didn't bring food, like I said I would. I didn't even take off my coat when I sat down on her bed. Knowing full well something had to be wrong, I looked her dead in the eye and said, "Did you talk to John today?"

She looked straight back and without skipping a beat said, "No."

I responded with, "Not at all?" to which she said, "Well, I called to tell him that we couldn't talk anymore but he didn't answer."

I stood up, looked her dead in the eye and said, "You are a f&$(8$ liar. Give me my ring back."

She started crying and saying she was sorry.

I took my ring, grabbed all the things I gave her that had sentimental value and started walking out the door. She kept saying she was sorry and to wait. I stopped, and in a moment of lost self-control, I yelled, "Sorry just isn't going to effing cut it. You lie. You sneak behind my back talking to other guys. You say it's just about us but you end our conversations because you say you are tired and going to bed and then call him and talk until 5 in the morning. YOU EFFING LIE," to which she said I scared her and to get out of her house. I told her if I walk out that door, I'm never coming back. She said we aren't ever going to resolve this tonight and just let me go. I waited 5 minutes at the front door, but she never came so I went home.

The next day at work, I lost total control of my emotions, up down, left and right. I could not reign it in. This was so uncharacteristic. It freaked me out. It made me physically sick to the point I was sent home as not fit for duty because they thought I had the flu. I didn't give them any reason to think otherwise. If they knew a relationship had me so unhinged, I don't even want to think what the fall-out would be. I went home, took a cold shower, tried but failed to eat and then called my mother. If there's one person I could open up to, it would be her I reasoned. She told me "Once trust is lost like that, it will always be in the back of your head."

Despite the negativity I deal with on a daily basis, I remain positive and truly believe that everyone has a good side. People make mistakes, and if they can understand and correct what they did wrong, everyone deserves a second chance. Love is forgiveness after all, right? Man was that naive. My dumb arse grabbed my ring and went over to her house to forgive her.

She had been texting and calling all day, saying she was sorry and she was wrong. She panicked when I asked her about the calls and she didn't want to make me mad after we had such an honest and good conversation. She said we had finally started mending the strain on our relationship. I ate it all up and that's where I gave in to the second chance mentality.

I'd like to note that in the past, I've never forgiven dishonesty and the disrespect associated with it. It's just one of those things that is very important to me and unforgivable, but this girl had me twisted all around.

I showed up unannounced and she was shocked. I was supposed to be at work all day after all. She had obviously been crying and she broke down instantly upon seeing me and just held on to me for dear life. My heart melted. We sat down and I started talking. I told her that when I first gave her that ring that I meant what I said, I wanted to spend the rest of my life with her and was committed to us no matter what it takes. At that point, her grandmother walked in the front door. My ex apologized and said she had to go with her to an appointment and had completely forgotten. I was ok with that. I did show up unannounced after all. We promised to meet up after and just talk.

Well six hours later and nothing. I contacted her and she said that the fact I showed up was just shocking and that she thinks that I will always hold this against her, always question her, etc. I told her she was right and I would if she didn't do anything to make me think otherwise.

She said she wasn't willing to give up her friendship with John because she didn't think she did anything wrong. I went and got my ring back and gave back everything she ever game me. She didn't want to face me so I had to drop it off at her parent's place of business and initiated no contact.

She FREAKED out when she got all the stuff I had left with her mom. Over the next 48 hours, it was message after message, call after call, leaving voicemails saying I love you and miss you, and asking me how I could just cut her out. I caved in on the third day, and it was just a back and forth of me trying to fix it and her saying she wanted to, but doing nothing to actually fix it. I got frustrated and we ultimately decided to spend some time apart, evaluate ourselves, and give it a try in a few weeks.

Well, over the next few days I found out the extent of her deception and betrayal went far beyond phone calls. It was intimate and they were definitely more than just friends. I ended it by telling her she was a lying bit@# before she hung up on me and that was the last I talked to her. That was about 20 days ago.

Like I said, I went back and evaluated everything that happened over the entire time we were together. I discovered some more deceit when someone sent me some anonymous emails from her phone regarding emails sent between her and others during our relationship. I'm pretty sure I know who it was, a coworker of hers that I'd known for a long time that she had screwed over pretty badly, but I'll never be able to prove it or I would buy them a beer for opening my eyes to who she really is.

I learned that this is a pattern of hers. She always has someone waiting in the wings. Always keeping and opening new options. When things go wrong, she establishes the foundations of a new relationship and just jumps ship. She did it to boyfriend A to B, then B to C, then C with me. The only reason she panicked was because her new relationship wasn't firmly established yet. It wasn't a sure thing yet. I caught her in the act and exposed her game before she could dump me and that threw a huge wrench in how she operates. By the time I ended it, once and for all, she was set with John and has since just disappeared. I got the last word and since, it's been No Contact.

I know that the love I had was an illusion. I loved what I thought was her and not the real person. In my mind, I've already let go and logically, I want nothing to do with her. But something is missing. I never really thought heartache was a real thing but I can assure you now that it is. There's a tightness in my chest that just won't go away. It makes it difficult to breathe, eat, or sleep. It's constant.

I've done everything I can think of to help myself move on. I've been hitting the gym. I started to really do it to help when things first started to go south in November. I've lost almost 25 lbs. I'm in the best shape of my life. I went out and bought myself some new clothes, reorganized all of my things, spent time with friends, and reconnected with a lot of friends I lost touch with because of her. But in the end, that's all just a quick fix. It only makes me feel better for a short time. There are only so many times in a day you can go to the gym, only so much you can do to move around your house, you know?

The worst part is that this all came as a complete shock. One lie caused me to look into everything and soon everything just exploded. I couldn't prepare. I reacted and I know my reaction was the right one, but still, to be with someone so long, always have them texting and calling to absolute nothing is probably the worst. My phone is eerily quiet. I just check it a hundred times a day, not necessarily to see if she broke No Contact, but to see if anyone out there tried contacting me at all.

I've been through bad breakups. I've been cheated on before. I always look at it as one day at a time. You wake up and you are down but every day you feel better just a little bit sooner until you are back to being happy with you. But with this, everything seems to get worse and last longer. I can barely manage to eat anything. The only reason I eat is because I know I have to. I lay in bed at night, scared to close my eyes because I know I will dream about the good times or about how she just cut me out completely at the end.

I guess because integrity has always been a big part of my life, I don't understand the lies. I'm not a trusting person in the sense that I don't let people close to me easily. But as my friends would tell you, once I do let someone in, I trust them completely and they know that I would take a bullet for them without hesitation. Like I mentioned before, I handle emotions differently than a lot of others so I don't throw 'I love you' around like it's nothing. If I say it, I absolutely mean it with all of my being. It just kills me to know that she could say that to me and do what she did at the same time. Now she's happy and I'm miserable and I have to grieve about that too.

Again, I just feel lost. The traditional remedies don't help. Everyone says just keep doing what you are doing. Time is all that's left, but time isn't helping. It's making it worse. I made her a part of my life, included her in everything about me from the things I used to do to make myself feel better to taking her to the places I used to go to just escape and think when I was upset or angry or frustrated.

I'm trying to get out and do new things and meet new people. I've been going out to the bars at night with friends to distract myself (I'm not drinking, personally just not my thing) but that's now my scene. New hobbies bore me. I love my job, but I can't focus and almost my entire 13 hour shift is spent alone. Not focusing at what I do is definitely not conducive to coming home safe at night. My friends, like I said, are all in long term relationships and are set in their own routines so it gets dull doing the same things over and over again. I've tried to meet new people, but it's very hard not being a chatty person.

I'm beating myself up trying to show her I'm better than that. I'm trying to prove to myself that I'm not what she says about me. I'm forcing myself to stay up late even when I'm exhausted because she said I was always sleeping early. I'm going out and doing things I never did before even though I don't like to because it's the only thing I didn't do with her. I'm writing long winded messages on the Internet to strangers. I'm not being me. I'm not unhappy with me. I'm actually very proud of what I've accomplished in my life. I know I have a great future ahead of me and that I have a lot to offer.

I'm no idiot. I know I'm missing the feelings I had in the relationship, not her. She's not on that pedestal any more. In fact, I made my list of the good vs. the bad. After looking at it, I tossed it in my fireplace. The facts speak for themselves, and the very thought of who she is makes me sick.

Key Themes

I hope you see the key themes emerging through everyone's story, such as gaslighting, cheating, projection, yelling, belittling and push/pull behavior that you've most likely experienced firsthand in your relationship. Narcissists isolate you from your friends and family as a way to obtain more control over you.

You may also have noticed Andre, Andy and Ray all mention that when their focus shifted from the narcissist in the slightest bit or they weren't paying enough attention to them, the narcissist would rage or punish them.

The realization in my marriage that my ex-husband's narcissism was pathological came while I was pursuing my Master's degree. We had been married close to 5 years at this point and I was busy with my studies, which I thought he supported. I asked him why he never wanted to spend time with me when I was free, and he answered by telling me it was because I no longer paid enough attention to what he was reading or what he was interested in.

Therefore, I made it a point to pay particular attention to what he was reading when we went to bed that night. The irony in it all is that he was reading Christopher Lasch's book "The Culture of Narcissism – American Life in an Age of Diminishing Expectations."

It was at that moment the lightbulb in my head finally went off and I remembered he had joked about being a narcissist when we first started dating. Or at least, I thought it was just a lighthearted joke. Unfortunately, I was too naive and too smitten with him to take it seriously and dismissed it as something that just made him that much more artsy and eccentric at the time.

This is precisely why sharing your story and journaling is so critical to our self-care and recovery. When we do this, it allows us to identify themes and trends in someone else's behavior....even in our own, which can help us immensely. As you can see, all of these stories have similar key themes with regards to the narcissist's behavior and how each person responded with self-blame and doubt. Some even commented that they felt like they weren't good enough and blamed themselves for the demise of the relationship. This is precisely what the narcissist counts on. They condition us to doubt ourselves so we stay dependent on them. However, we must remember that it's nothing more than manipulation. Narcissists are sadistic and sadly enjoy causing others to suffer. Some even say that they get off on it.

It's critical for you to confront the trauma you experienced and process the emotions that are a direct result of the pain you endured. We cannot repress our feelings and we must confront what happened to us. If we do not, we will remain stuck. Sharing your story, even if it's only privately in a journal, is so important to your recovery.

"There is no coming to consciousness without pain." -Carl Jung

Eckhart Tolle refers to this state of being as the "Pain Body." In his groundbreaking book, "The Power of Now," Tolle explains how the Pain Body is actually afraid of the light of consciousness. Its survival is dependent on your unconscious fear of facing the pain that lives inside you. In other words, you will remain in a state of pain, darkness or unhappiness as long as you continue to lie to yourself and deny your reality. Resistance is what keeps us stuck in the unconscious realm. Tolle believes the more you resist the present moment, the more pain you create within yourself. [2]

In my opinion, the only true path to enlightenment is to drop all inner resistance and be honest with ourselves. We must allow ourselves to feel our feelings and not be ashamed. When you give a feeling full expression, it diminishes its power and brings about a transformation. Once you acknowledge and express the feeling, it causes the feeling to subside, as it can't go on forever.

Fortunately, science is now confirming such statements. Recent research confirms that crying is good for us because it cleanses our system of toxins and waste, reduces tension and increases our body's ability to heal itself.

Alan Wolfelt Ph.D., a professor at the University of Colorado Medical School, has measured the chemical benefits of crying and states: "In my clinical experience with thousands of mourners, I have observed changes in physical (appearance) following the expression of tears...Not only do people feel better after crying; they also look better."

The kind of tears our eyes produce for moisture to remove dust or sand and the kind that we produce by crying are chemically different. Crying tears are made-up of manganese. In fact, crying tears are thirty times richer in manganese than blood is, for example. According to biochemists, manganese is only one of three chemicals that are stored up by stress and flushed out by a good cry.

In the school of nursing at Marquette University, nurses are asked not to immediately provide tranquilizers to weeping patients. Instead, they are encouraged to allow the tears to do their own therapeutic work.

Dr. Margaret Crepeau, professor of nursing at Marquette states: "Laughter and tears are two inherent natural medicines whereby we can reduce duress, let out negative feelings and recharge. They truly are the body's own best resources."

Unfortunately, many people are socialized and brought up to believe that we shouldn't express our emotions. We learn to repress our feelings as if they are a sign of insecurity or weakness. In my opinion, this is disastrous to our well-being.

"Primal Scream Therapy" is a trauma-based psychotherapy created by Arthur Janov, who believes neurosis is caused by the repressed pain of childhood trauma. Janov argues that unresolved pain can be brought to conscious awareness by re-experiencing painful childhood feelings or events and fully expressing the resulting pain during therapy. Janov believes this type of therapy resolves pain from the past. Primal therapy first became influential in the early 1970s, after the publication of Janov's first book, "The Primal Scream."

Janov used Primal Scream Therapy to help patients resolve childhood pain by processing their emotions, integrating them and thus, becoming *real*. The goal of his therapy is to lessen or eliminate the hold early trauma exerts on adult life.

As we know, trauma can be experienced at any point in one's life. In a relationship with a narcissist, emotional abuse causes trauma. Emotional abuse is much harder to pinpoint than physical abuse because there are no visible scars. However, emotional abuse is just as real as any other type of abuse and causes the same kind of emotional trauma. The resulting trauma you experienced cannot be ignored. Just like a physical wound, it must be dealt with and tended to in order to heal.

Janov states that neurosis is the result of suppressed pain, which is the result of trauma. According to Janov, the only way to reverse neurosis is for the patient to confront their trauma and express the emotions that occurred at that time. I agree and believe that we must confront these experiences and process our feelings about what occurred in order to move on.

John Lennon said that his Primal Scream Therapy sessions with Arthur Janov in 1970 were the catalyst for his most emotionally bare album, "John Lennon/Plastic Ono Band." I love what Lennon had to say about Primal Scream Therapy in this Howard Smith Radio Interview:

"There's no way of describing it, it all sounds so straight just talking about it, what you actually do is cry. Instead of penting up emotion, or pain, feel it rather than putting it away for some rainy day..... I think everybody's blocked, I haven't met anybody that isn't a complete blockage of pain from childhood, from birth on...... It's like somewhere along the line we were switched off not to feel things, like for instance, crying, men crying and women being very girlish or whatever it is, somewhere you have to switch into a role and this therapy gives you back the switch, locate it and switch back into feeling just as a human being, not as a male or a female or as a famous person or not famous person, they switch you back to being a baby and therefore you feel as a child does, but it's something we forget because there's so much pressure and pain and whatever it is that is life, everyday life, that we gradually switch off over the years. All the generation gap crap is that the older people are more dead, as the years go by the pain doesn't go away, the pain of living, you have to kill yourself to survive. This allows you to live and survive without killing yourself."

CHAPTER 3

NO CONTACT

As you heard from those who shared their story, the only way to break free from a narcissist is to establish and maintain a rule of No Contact. You must treat your narcissist as if you are breaking a toxic drug habit. You must realize that she has become like a drug to you.

Just as she needs others to validate her existence, she has now programmed you to believe you need her in order to survive. But, you do not need her and you're better off without her in your life. You may not feel that way right now, but that's simply because you're addicted to her in an unhealthy way.

A narcissist programs you to question yourself....question everything about yourself, in fact. That is their goal from the very beginning. The narcissist knows if she can cause you to doubt yourself, you will become dependent on her for validation and keep coming back. It is critical that you understand you will never get over a narcissist if you go back or remain in contact with her in any way or capacity. As you learned in the stories shared here, you should never go back. You can and will deprogram from her, but only once you establish No Contact. You must cut off all contact with her in order to break free.

No Contact means just that.....you must have absolutely NO CONTACT with your narcissist. In other words:

No personal visits

No phone calls, incoming or outgoing

Do not answer her calls

Block her phone number

If she uses a different number and you do answer, hang up immediately

No emails, incoming or outgoing. Delete before reading

No texts, incoming or outgoing. Delete before reading

No Facebook or dating websites where she may be found

Do not look for her on the Internet

Do not Google her name

Do not talk to her friends or family. Avoid these conversations at all costs

Delete and destroy any reminders of her

Do not save emails, letters or photos

Everything must go!

The act of cleaning or disposing of certain articles is internally cleansing. It helps clear away the memories associated with the relationship. Remove tangible reminders of your narcissist, such as framed photos or albums. This will help you 'cut the chords' of connection, so to speak. It is the connection that is so intense. They have their hooks in us deep. Any physical or visual exercise you can perform to help you cut off your connection with your narcissist is one I highly recommend.

A narcissist will contact you with the hope that you will return in a state of panic because she has led you to believe you cannot exist on your own. She wants to convince you that you need her in order to survive. The irony in all of this is that the narcissist is the one who needs YOU in order to feel alive, but she has done a brilliant job of PROJECTING her issues onto you so you are the one who feels dependent on her now.

Clearly, when one is co-parenting with a narcissist, No Contact is somewhat tricky. Where children are involved, the goal of No Contact is to refrain from engaging in any type of communication with her above and beyond what is necessary for your children's well-being. Aside from this, you should not have any contact with her whatsoever. She has already taken enough from you. Do not continue to let her take more. Your days of being the doormat and servant to the narcissist are over.

Please remember No Contact is the only way to begin the process of deprogramming from a narcissist. Unless you physically detach and disconnect from the narcissist, they will still have a hold over you.

"You cannot solve a problem from the same consciousness that created it." -Albert Einstein

Having any type of contact with the narcissist while trying to break free will only keep you stuck under her spell. Creating distance is the only way to gain perspective and see things as they truly are. We must break contact in order to really assess the situation.

It is this distance that allows us to look at things from the perspective of a "PLAYER" considering their next move versus a "PAWN" waiting to be played.

We often do not realize how horribly they treated us until we physically remove ourselves from their proximity. Any contact with them keeps us under their influence, which makes it more difficult to recognize what is going on. It is only once we pull away completely and deprogram that we begin to see the extent of the emotional abuse we suffered. We are amazed by what we tolerated. This just goes to show how addicted we were.

We have the ability to get in touch with ourselves again. They do not. We cannot let them drag us down into their miserable world of nonexistence. The longer we are in contact with them, the longer it takes to deprogram from them. The only way to successfully start to deprogram is to establish No Contact as soon as possible.

NarcSpeak

Narcissists say the strangest things and we are often left scratching our heads trying to make sense of the senseless. Remember, narcissists are not normal. They don't think like we do. They don't speak normally either. Most of what they say is meant to confuse us, throw us off and manipulate us. They use backward-talk, projection, martyrdom and almost ALWAYS provoke us to respond in a manner they can then use against us. They often use NLP, NeuroLinguistic Programming, used in sales, marketing, politics and seduction/mind control. They are brilliant manipulators.

We call it "NarcSpeak" in our support group and you should be aware of this tactic so you can recognize when it's occurring. Below are common narcissistic comments that have been translated to show their true meaning.

The first comment in **bold** is **the narcissist speaking**

The second comment in ALL CAPS is the TRANSLATION

I feel a sort of kinship with you.

YOU'RE A GREAT TARGET. I'M LINING YOU UP AS MY NEXT VICTIM. WONDER IF YOU'LL FALL FOR THE "YOU'RE MY SOULMATE" LINE?

I have finally met my match.

THIS LINE WORKS REALLY WELL SO I SAY IT TO EVERY ONE OF MY TARGETS... LET'S HOPE THEY NEVER MEET AND SHARE NOTES!

I see something in you.

I CAN EXPLOIT, USE AND ABUSE YOU FOR MY OWN NEEDS. YOU HAVE A LOT TO OFFER!

I need to hear your voice.

I NEED TO HEAR YOU TELL ME HOW PERFECT, WONDERFUL AND SMART I AM. I NEED YOU TO STROKE MY EGO.

I value you.

YOU'RE GREAT NARCISSISTIC SUPPLY AND YOU MAKE ME LOOK REALLY GOOD TO OTHERS.

Maybe I am not the right person for you.

I AM GOING TO "SOW THE SEEDS OF DOUBT" IN YOU SO THAT YOU WILL WORK HARDER TO MAKE ME HAPPY AND PLEASE ME ME ME!

I'm just trying to take care of myself.

MYSELF BEING THE OPERATIVE WORD HERE BECAUSE I AM THE ONLY ONE WHO MATTERS. WHY SHOULD I TAKE CARE OF MY RELATIONSHIP? I AM SO WONDERFUL THAT I CAN FIND ANOTHER TARGET EASILY!

It's not all about you, you know...

RIGHT, BECAUSE IT'S ALL ABOUT ME ME ME ME ME!!!!!

Have you always been like this?
IF I MAKE YOU FEEL BAD ABOUT YOURSELF, YOU WILL FEAR BEING
ALONE AND WILL NEVER FIGURE OUT THAT I AM THE ONE WHO IS
DISTURBED, SICK AND INHUMAN.

Who takes care of you better than I do?
I WANT YOU TO THINK YOU CAN'T TAKE CARE OF YOURSELF SO YOU
WILL BECOME DEPENDENT ON ME. I'M GOING TO TAKE OVER YOUR
LIFE, TURN YOU INTO MY PUPPET AND HAVE SOME FUN!

You took that out of context.
DAMN, YOU'RE ON TO ME. I NEED TO MAKE YOU THINK YOU'RE
LOSING YOUR MIND AND IMAGINING THINGS. I WILL DENY
EVERYTHING I SAID.

**It's like walking on eggshells living with you... I never know
what mood you will be in next.**
PROJECTION! TOTAL PROJECTION!!

If you really love me, you would understand me.
YOU NEED TO ANTICIPATE MY NEEDS BETTER! I EQUATE GETTING
EXACTLY WHAT I WANT WITH SOMEONE'S LOVE.

Think of our children and what this is doing to them.
I'LL USE ANYTHING TO GUILT TRIP YOU AND HAVE NO SHAME USING
OUR CHILDREN AS PAWNS.

I think I'm a really good person for you to know.
I'M GOING TO SUCK YOU DRY AND TAKE YOU FOR ALL YOU'RE
WORTH!

No one knows you better than I do.
NO ONE WILL BE ABLE TO MANIPULATE YOU THE WAY I DO.

I will never change.
I DON'T SEE ANY REASON TO CHANGE. I'M PERFECT.

You need someone to tell you what to do.
I WANT YOU TO FEEL SO DEPENDENT AND INCOMPETENT YOU HAVE TO ASK MY PERMISSION TO BREATHE. I CONTROL YOUR REALITY AND YOUR LIFE!

I'll take care of it. I have to take care of everything.
I WANT YOU TO BELIEVE YOU CAN'T DO ANYTHING RIGHT. I AM NOT GOING TO ALLOW YOU TO HAVE AN INDEPENDENT THOUGHT BECAUSE I NEED TO KEEP YOU DEPENDENT ON ME.

You read too much into everything.
YOU'RE GETTING CLOSE TO FIGURING ME OUT. DAMN YOU!

You know that's not what I meant to say, so stop twisting my words.
TWISTING WORDS IS MY THING!!!

I'm not going to get into this right now!
YOU'RE CATCHING ON TO ME... I AM GOING TO SHAME DUMP AND GUILT-TRIP YOU SO YOU WILL STOP QUESTIONING ME.

You were abusive to me.
(PROJECTION) I WAS ABUSIVE TO YOU AND I DIDN'T LIKE YOU CALLING ME ON IT. I SHOULD BE ABLE TO TREAT YOU HOWEVER I WANT WITH NO CONSEQUENCES.

You were not appreciative of all I did for you.
WHICH IS NOTHING BUT MANIPULATE, AND NO MATTER WHAT YOU DID FOR ME, IT WOULD NEVER BE ENOUGH.

What's so hard about throwing your arms around me?
I DESERVE LOVE, AFFECTION AND ADORATION. WHY AREN'T YOU WORSHIPPING ME?!

I didn't want to make you paranoid.
WHAT I REALLY DIDN'T WANT WAS FOR YOU TO FIND OUT! DAMN YOU!

You have commitment issues.
YOU WON'T IGNORE THE WAY I USE AND EXPLOIT YOU. YOU WANT A REAL, HONEST, HUMAN RELATIONSHIP. I AM NOT HUMAN, BUT I'LL TELL YOU THAT YOU'RE THE ONE WITH ISSUES.

You always think you're right and never back down.
YOU'RE GETTING WAY TOO SMART FOR ME - HOW I CAN MAKE YOU DOUBT YOURSELF? OH YEAH...I KNOW...BLAME YOU FOR DEFENDING YOURSELF!

Would I lie to you?
I ALWAYS LIE TO YOU, EVERYONE ELSE AND EVEN MYSELF.

Why couldn't you have just agreed to disagree?
WHY COULDN'T YOU HAVE LET ME WIN AND DO WHATEVER I WANT?

I left you because of the way you treated me.
I LEFT BECAUSE YOU STARTED TO FIGURE ME OUT.

We argued all the time.
YOU WOULDN'T LET ME WALK ALL OVER YOU!

You are just too difficult.
YOU ARE TOO SMART AND STARTING TO WAKE UP FROM THE MIND CONTROL.

Your expectations are unreasonable.
I CAN'T GIVE YOU WHAT YOU WANT BECAUSE I AM NOT HUMAN.
LET'S MAKE THIS YOUR FAULT BY TELLING YOU THAT YOUR
EXPECTATIONS ARE TOO HIGH.

Good luck finding someone who will put up with you.
I WANT YOUR SELF-ESTEEM TO BE NON-EXISTENT SO EVEN WHEN
I'M GONE MY WORDS CONTROL YOUR MIND FOREVER!

Your character will never change.
HOW DARE YOU BE STRONG ENOUGH TO RIP OFF MY MASK!

You don't pay attention to me anymore.
IT'S ALL ABOUT ME AND YOU STOPPED GIVING ME SUPPLY AND
WORSHIPPING THE GROUND I WALK ON.

Talking to you is to fight with you.
I LOVE FIGHTING & DRAMA - I LIVE FOR IT! I CREATE CHAOS - IT
MAKES ME FEEL POWERFUL!

Stop attacking me.
I DON'T LIKE BEING HELD ACCOUNTABLE FOR ANYTHING! HOW
DARE YOU QUESTION ME AND RIP MY FALSE MASK OFF!

I fear we are going to have a big misunderstanding and never talk again.
I'M GOING TO CREATE A SITUATION THAT JUSTIFIES ME DISCARDING
AND DEVALUING YOU AND MAKE YOU BELIEVE IT'S YOUR FAULT - IT
WILL MAKE YOUR HEAD SPIN!

I will always love you.
I KNOW SAYING THAT "LOVE" WORD GETS ME WHAT I WANT SO I'LL
SAY IT EVEN THOUGH I AM CLUELESS AS TO WHAT IT REALLY
MEANS.

We will always be attracted to each other.

I'LL PLANT THIS ONE IN YOUR BRAIN TO ENSURE I CAN COME
AROUND AND SLEEP WITH YOU WHENEVER I WANT.

I guess this relationship has not been healthy for you.

WOW I FEEL SO GOOD INSIDE KNOWING HOW BAD I MESSED YOU
UP. I AM SO POWERFUL! ME ME ME!!

I'm gonna see you again, we have mutual friends.

I AM GONNA STALK YOU AND FOLLOW YOU AND HARASS YOU SO
BUCKLE UP, BABY!

Why are you being like this?

WHY ARE YOU ASKING ME TO BE HUMAN AND HAVE FEELINGS?

You drag me down.

YOU ARE TOO MUCH REALITY FOR ME... I AM SPECIAL AND YOU ARE
NOT WORSHIPPING ME THE WAY I SHOULD BE WORSHIPPED RIGHT
NOW SO I HAVE NO USE FOR YOU.

I need to be myself.

I AM OFF TO FIND SOME NEW PREY

CHAPTER 4

WHAT'S HAPPENING TO ME?

Narcissists use several different methods of coercion in order to control you. She may have threatened, degraded, shifted blame, criticized, manipulated, verbally assaulted, dominated, blackmailed, withdrew, withheld love and affection and gaslighted in an effort to make you feel as though you were going crazy.

She denied that events ever occurred or certain things were said. As a result, you doubt what you're hearing and seeing to the point that you begin to question your sanity. This is exactly what the narcissist set out to do. She wants you to believe you are imagining things and have some kind of mental illness or faulty memory.

When we doubt our perception of reality, the narcissist is able to control us knowing we are dependent on them for the truth. A narcissist wants us to believe we have problems and issues only they can understand and are willing to tolerate. By doing this, we start to feel unlovable, paranoid and doubtful, which ensures our dependence on them and subsequent ability to control us.

Cognitive Dissonance

When you first establish No Contact, it's important to understand that your mind will experience what's called Cognitive Dissonance, which is the difficulty of trying to hold two opposing thoughts or beliefs at the same time.

Cognitive Dissonance leads to obsessive, intrusive thoughts that impede our ability to concentrate, work, sleep, eat or function. It can often feel like we are in a fog or haze of some kind. Our mind is not functioning properly because we have experienced psychological trauma.

We obsess because we are trying to make sense of a situation that makes no sense. How can I love something that I also hate? How can I be crazy in love with this person, but despise her at the same time? We remember the wonderful times, the good times and the person we thought we fell in love with and we miss them. We wonder what happened to them. Where did they go? Why did they disappear? What did I do wrong?

While we're remembering this person who no longer seems to exist, we are grappling with a new person we no longer recognize, and we don't know how to feel about them. You ask yourself: How can she be good and bad? How can I love her and hate her? Trying to resolve this in your mind is very confusing and leads to Cognitive Dissonance, which impedes your ability to concentrate, work, sleep, eat or function.

We must remember that we did NOTHING wrong nor is there anything that can be done to bring this person back to us. The person we fell in love with is not who we thought they were at all. They never existed. We fell in love with an illusion. Narcissists are shallow, hollow and empty.

Realizing this person is NOT who you thought they were and NOT someone you want to be with is KEY to maintaining No Contact. Once you realize separation from the narcissist is a GOOD THING, you are on the path to true recovery.

Obsessive Thoughts

You should also expect to experience obsessive thoughts. This is because you have been programmed to doubt yourself and most likely experienced constant criticism and belittling from the narcissist. Obsessive-Compulsive Disorder is commonly referred to as the Doubting Disease.

We have also been conditioned in life to avoid pain and seek pleasure. As a result, we engage in obsessive thinking so we can avoid confronting the painful reality of our situation. We use the recurring thoughts to distract ourselves from what we really need to confront and process – our feelings.

Many of us avoid our feelings by identifying too much with our mind - we over-analyze and over-think everything. I know I am guilty of this, and Cognitive Dissonance contributes to this phenomenon. What we don't realize is that we are unconsciously obsessing in an attempt to avoid our pain. Instead of allowing ourselves to feel, we distract ourselves by getting caught up in obsessive ideation.

Obsessive thoughts are a reaction to anxiety that we feel. No one likes to feel anxiety, so we find ways to numb or decrease our anxiety. One way we do this is through engaging in obsessive-compulsive behavior. Just as one may use drugs or alcohol, one can use obsessive thoughts to avoid having to feel.

It took me a long time to figure this out, but when I did, it really opened my eyes. By obsessing, overanalyzing and staying 'in our head' we avoid having to really feel the emotions that are trying to pour out of us. Believe it or not, this is exactly what the narcissist is counting on. They want us to disconnect from ourselves so we remain dependent on them for survival.

When all we can do is obsess about our narcissist, it's near impossible to avoid responding when we hear from them. We become consumed with trying to figure them out. Although we have the knowledge we need to stay away, Cognitive Dissonance keeps us wondering if they are really all that bad. We want to give them another chance to prove us wrong, to prove that they really are capable of love.

Unfortunately, we learn the hard way that they will never change. Some of us need to learn this lesson more than once. Others can move on more quickly. It is my hope that by understanding why you obsess about your narcissist, it will help you stay away and move on more quickly.

Please remember when you are stuck in an obsessive-compulsive cycle of thought, you could be avoiding your feelings. By distracting yourself with mind rituals, you can easily forget about the emotions trying to surface inside you. Think about it, if you are engaged in obsessive thought and consumed with your mind, who has time to feel? Identifying with your mind allows you to avoid having to feel.

If you find yourself obsessing, I challenge you to ask yourself this question: What feeling am I trying to avoid right now?

You may find there is a very strong emotion you are avoiding. We have to stop being afraid to feel our feelings. We must learn not to elude our feelings with methods of distraction.

Post-Traumatic Stress Disorder

Along with Cognitive Dissonance and obsessive thoughts, you should be aware of the possibility that you may be suffering from Post-traumatic Stress Disorder (PTSD) as a result of the emotional abuse and psychological trauma you endured in your relationship with a narcissist.

According to the DSM-IV, PTSD occurs when:

A. The person has been exposed to a traumatic event in which both of the following have been present:

141

(1) the person experienced, witnessed, or was confronted with an event or events that involved actual or threatened death or serious injury, or a threat to the physical integrity of self or others

(2) the person's response involved intense fear, helplessness, or horror. Note: In children, this may be expressed instead by disorganized or agitated behavior.

B. The traumatic event is persistently re-experienced in one (or more) of the following ways:

(1) recurrent and intrusive distressing recollections of the event, including images, thoughts, or perceptions. Note: In young children, repetitive play may occur in which themes or aspects of the trauma are expressed.

(2) recurrent distressing dreams of the event. Note: In children, there may be frightening dreams without recognizable content.

(3) acting or feeling as if the traumatic event were recurring (includes a sense of reliving the experience, illusions, hallucinations, and dissociative flashback episodes, including those that occur upon awakening or when intoxicated). Note: In young children, trauma-specific reenactment may occur.

(4) intense psychological distress at exposure to internal or external cues that symbolize or resemble an aspect of the traumatic event.

(5) physiological reactivity on exposure to internal or external cues that symbolize or resemble an aspect of the traumatic event.

C. Persistent avoidance of stimuli associated with the trauma and numbing of general responsiveness (not present before the trauma), as indicated by three (or more) of the following:

(1) efforts to avoid thoughts, feelings, or conversations associated with the trauma

(2) efforts to avoid activities, places, or people that arouse recollections of the trauma

(3) inability to recall an important aspect of the trauma

(4) markedly diminished interest or participation in significant activities

(5) feeling of detachment or estrangement from others

(6) restricted range of affect (e.g., unable to have loving feelings)

(7) sense of a foreshortened future (e.g., does not expect to have a career, marriage, children, or a normal life span)

D. Persistent symptoms of increased arousal (not present before the trauma), as indicated by two (or more) of the following:

(1) difficulty falling or staying asleep
(2) irritability or outbursts of anger
(3) difficulty concentrating
(4) hypervigilance
(5) exaggerated startle response

E. Duration of the disturbance (symptoms in Criteria B, C, and D) is more than one month.

F. The disturbance causes clinically significant distress or impairment in social, occupational, or other important areas of functioning.

Specify if:

Acute: if duration of symptoms is less than 3 months

Chronic: if duration of symptoms is 3 months or more

With Delayed Onset: if onset of symptoms is at least 6 months after the stressor

PTSD is very serious and can be detrimental to your physical health if not treated. If you feel you are experiencing any of these symptoms, you should seek medical attention right away. Only a doctor can determine if you are experiencing PTSD and provide the proper medical attention you need in order to heal and move on.

CHAPTER 5

TAKE BACK CONTROL

The key for my recovery has been the realization that while I cannot always control what happens to me in life, I can control how I RESPOND to it. Harnessing the power I have to deprogram from a toxic relationship is what finally allowed me to heal and move on. I want to help you realize the same potential within yourself.

Retrain Your Brain

Our society is undergoing a revolution in mental health with the newfound knowledge that we can retrain our brain. Thanks to recent advances in science and technology, we now know that our brains are much more plastic (changeable) than we ever thought.

The concept of brain plasticity, known as Neuroplasticity, is one of the greatest scientific breakthroughs in recent times. This field of research has proven that our brain is not permanently hardwired, but rather able to change physically, chemically and anatomically in response to our thoughts, experience and behavior. [1]

The fact that we can alter and heal our brain by directing how we respond to stimuli is so reassuring. It is a step-by-step process and takes time, but we now know we can reverse the damage caused by emotional abuse and psychological trauma. As Dr. Frank Lawlis, author of "Retraining the Brain" states: "This is possibly as great a leap forward in public health as the discovery of antibiotics and vaccines." [2]

There are several methods on how to achieve this. Working with a Cognitive Behavioral Therapist (CBT) to retrain my brain is what finally helped me move on. In my opinion, Cognitive Behavioral Therapy (CBT) is the most effective form of treatment for retraining your brain.

Cognitive Behavioral Therapy (CBT) is a type of treatment that has been around for the last fifty years, but has just recently been gaining popularity. It's extremely helpful in managing Obsessive-Compulsive Disorder.

"Insanity is doing the same thing over and over, but expecting a different result." -**Albert Einstein**

We all are guilty of this at times. It's human nature. However, when it becomes a destructive pattern of behavior or repetitive negative thinking pattern, we must find a way to address it, right? CBT is exactly what is required in order to change this kind of obsessive-compulsive behavior.

Exposure Response Prevention (ERP) is the most common treatment in CBT and what it does is retrain your brain to respond differently to stimuli so you can stop engaging in self-destructive behavior. The idea being that responding differently will bring about a more positive result.

Cognitive therapy teaches us not to give others the power to upset us. We can easily allow other people or events to de-rail us and cause us great unhappiness. However, remember, it is not about what happens to us but how we RESPOND to it that matters, right?

CBT is a 'doing' therapy whereby the licensed therapist takes you through different mental exercises in an effort to help retrain your brain. This therapy is not easy as the exercises can be difficult and anxiety provoking at times, but it is incredibly effective.

CBT is based on the belief that emotional disturbance is caused by distorted or irrational reasoning. Humans can be influenced to think illogically. This warped way of thinking can be acquired at any point in someone's life.

Obviously, as a result of the abusive relationship we were in, we were influenced to think illogically and doubt ourselves. We no longer trust our judgment and are experiencing severe anxiety. We have been brainwashed by our narcissist and need to deprogram from them. In my opinion, Cognitive Behavioral Therapy (CBT) is the most effective form of treatment for retraining your brain.

I do not suggest anyone endure the pain of recovering from a narcissist alone. I encourage you to seek professional help and attend support group meetings in your area if available. Our support group is intended to assist you in your recovery, but certainly not meant to replace real therapy from a licensed mental health professional.

The most important thing to recognize when retraining your brain is that you are currently in a state of major anxiety. It is this anxiety that causes you to remain stuck and unable to focus on anything productive. You must acknowledge that you no longer want to remain in this negative pattern of thinking and will consciously make an effort to break free from it.

Webster defines anxiety as: "an abnormal and overwhelming sense of apprehension and fear often marked by physiological signs (as sweating, tension, and increased pulse), by doubt concerning the reality and nature of the threat, and by self-doubt about one's capacity to cope with it."

The key to retraining your brain is the ability to learn how to manage and cope with anxiety. It all comes down again to:

HOW YOU RESPOND

How you RESPOND to anxiety determines your ability to manage it. Everyone experiences anxiety. It is part of the human condition. 70 percent of adults report experiencing it daily and 30 percent report their anxiety levels are constant.[3]

"Things don't change. You change your way of looking at it, that's all." -Carlos Casteneda

Unfortunately, we are currently in a heightened state of constant anxiety as a result of the emotional abuse we experienced in a toxic relationship. We need to focus on retraining our brain. We know that heightened and prolonged trauma can lead to cognitive dissonance, obsessive-compulsive disorder, post-traumatic stress disorder, panic attacks and other phobias.

The key to retraining our brain is to: DESENSITIZE OURSELVES by controlling HOW WE RESPOND to anxiety in our lives.

"We are born into this world unarmed – our mind is our only weapon." -Ayn Rand

Manage Obsessive Thoughts

Here is what is happening in your mind when you experience anxiety:

Fear and stress trigger anxiety, which create noise and chaos that your brain cannot resolve. It is this noise that keeps you stuck and spinning in obsessive thought. The key to stop obsessing is to prevent yourself from responding to the thoughts that cause you to obsess in the first place. You see, obsessive thoughts are a direct result of anxiety.

Compulsions are what we do to in an attempt to try to reduce the anxiety....hence...obsessive-compulsive behavior.

Unfortunately, we think engaging in a compulsive behavior will lessen the anxiety, and it might initially, but it is only temporary. In fact, responding only increases the anxiety in the long run. Why? Because responding to the anxiety or obsessive thought in any way, shape or form only intensifies it. It validates it. It reinforces it and gives it power. We must not validate the unhealthy thoughts.

You can observe the thoughts, but do not judge. Do not try to wish the thoughts away either because it will only cause you to think of them more. Do not fight your thoughts. To do so only creates more obsessive thought. Allow your thoughts to happen, but do not validate or judge them in any way. Laugh at the thoughts, dismiss them, but do not fight them off. Instead, simply observe, but do not judge or respond to them. To ignore them decreases their power.

Please allow me to forewarn you that I am going to be purposively redundant in this upcoming section, but understand I simply want to be sure you realize the incredible power you have to manage your thoughts.

The key is not to control WHAT you think (that is impossible).

The key is to control HOW YOU RESPOND to what you think.

The key to managing all anxiety is learning how to RESPOND to it.

For example, we have an anxiety provoking thought....

We have a CHOICE in how we RESPOND to it...

We can judge and analyze the thought, thereby giving it significance and power, causing our mind to obsess and get stuck there...

Or

We do not judge or analyze the thought at all, thereby desensitizing ourselves to it and allowing our mind to move on.....

It is all in how we RESPOND

OBSESSIVE THOUGHT OR ANXIETY OCCURS....

RESPOND BY OBSERVING IT AND NOT JUDGING IT

= RELEASE IT & MOVE ON

OBSESSIVE THOUGHT OR ANXIETY OCCURS....

RESPOND BY JUDGING IT AND ANALYZING IT

= OBSESS MORE & GET STUCK

By controlling how we respond to our anxiety, we control our ability to manage it. For example, if we respond by trying to avoid it, we only increase the power and hold the thought has over us. However, if we respond with no judgment, and simply acknowledge it as OCD, we slowly desensitize ourselves to it, thereby lessening the control it has over us.

Simply observe the thought and realize that thoughts do not define you and are not a part of you. They are simply thoughts. Look at the obsessive thoughts as a separate entity and you will be able to distance yourself from them. The thoughts will always come. We have no control over that. Do not fight that. If you fight that, you're only setting yourself up for failure. It's like telling people not to look at the 'elephant' in the room. Everyone is going to look, right?

Do not fight the thoughts or tell yourself not to think of them. Instead, you simply control how you RESPOND to the thoughts when they occur......because trust me, they will occur. You cannot prevent yourself from thinking thoughts. You can only control how you RESPOND to your thoughts. In my opinion, that is the fundamental key to successfully managing anxiety.

Everyone gets unwanted, intrusive thoughts. Yes, everyone. However, those who have not been emotionally abused do not over-analyze or judge these thoughts the way we do. They let random thoughts roll-off of them.

Unfortunately, this has become difficult for us to do because we are experiencing Cognitive Dissonance and possibly PTSD. As a result, we over-analyze and obsess about every little thought that pops into our mind. As I've said before, this is precisely what the narcissist counts on. If we feel paralyzed to act, confused by our thoughts and doubtful, we will never leave them. This is where the narcissist wants us... under their control... asking them to clarify what is truth and what is reality.

I am often asked by readers if obsessing about their narcissist means they belong together. Absolutely not! Thoughts of your narcissist do not mean you still love her, need her or should be with her. Thoughts of your narcissist simply mean she has managed to manipulate you to obsess over her and should be further proof that you need to deprogram from her.

You must accept that you will have thoughts in the future about your narcissist that you would rather not have. They were a significant part of your life. It is natural to still think about her. In fact, it would be unnatural if you never thought of her.

You cannot control thoughts that come to mind. Memory is memory. Once created, it cannot be erased. However, the good news is you can control how you will RESPOND to the thoughts that pop into your head and that is the key to reducing your anxiety.

You must not fight off thoughts of your narcissist because they are going to arise. The key is not to judge the thoughts or respond to the thoughts when they do arise.

If you respond to the thoughts in any other way but indifference, you give them power and start the cycle of obsessive ideation.

So the key is not to fight the thoughts. Simply observe the thoughts. It is how you RESPOND to the thoughts that matter.

You can even try not to think of them as your own thoughts but simply 'intrusive thoughts' that prevent you from getting in touch with yourself. Looking at them in this way is helpful because the less you identify with the thoughts, the more quickly you can get back to your real self. The obsessive thoughts are just trying to distract you from feeling what you need to feel and doing what you need to do.

We can take back control. We can deprogram and begin to trust ourselves again. A member of our support group put it very well when she said:

"It's ok to revisit places we have been in our lives (in our minds) but just don't throw out the anchor and stay there."

And you know what the anchor is? You know what causes you to get stuck?

When you:

JUDGE OR ANALYZE the thoughts.

The MOMENT you judge or analyze your thoughts is the MOMENT you.....

ANCHOR THEM & GET STUCK.

The longer you hold the anxiety, the heavier it will feel.

Thoughts are random. They don't define us. We cannot control them. They don't mean anything. There is no hidden or deeper meaning behind crazy thoughts or memories. In fact, some thoughts may even frighten you, but they are nothing more than white noise trying to distract you from having a REAL RELATIONSHIP with YOURSELF.

We will always have intrusive, unwanted thoughts. Everyone does. The good news is that we have a choice in how we RESPOND to these thoughts. Remember, life is not about what happens to us, it is how we RESPOND that matters.

Practicing this has helped me tremendously. I finally have peace of mind I never thought was possible. The thoughts still come, but by choosing how I will respond to these thoughts, I have reduced the power and the hold they have over me. I prevent myself from responding to the thoughts in any way that will intensify their strength.

They are only thoughts after all. Thoughts cannot hurt me, but how I RESPOND to my thoughts can hurt me. Being paralyzed with anxiety over thoughts is no way to live life. It prohibits us from truly living and experiencing all life has to offer.

Thought Replacement

At one time, we thought there was a single memory system in the brain. Thanks to recent advances in science and technology, we now know that memories are formed in a variety of systems and can easily be divided into two major categories:

Conscious Memory (i.e. explicit factual memory systems)

and

Unconscious or Subconscious Memory (i.e implicit emotional memory systems)

We know that narcissists operate only in a world of explicit memory where emotions are non-existent. They have excellent explicit memory, which includes the details, the how to, when, where, and what of a situation or event. However, they have horrible implicit memory, which is always triggered by an emotion via a sense of smell, touch, taste, etc. As discussed earlier, narcissists are incapable of bringing forth emotional memories, only factual memories.

It is important to understand the difference between the two types of memory when trying to get over a narcissist. The reason is simple. Our emotional memory is extremely powerful and by learning how to harness its power, we can dramatically improve our quality of life.

We respond to events in our life based on images and memories we have stored in our subconscious. We can change how we respond to certain events in our life by engaging our subconscious. I believe our subconscious drives all of our behavior. Therefore, learning how to tap into its power has amazing benefits.

To give you an idea of how powerful the subconscious is, compare it to the rate at which we speak. Our subconscious operates at a rate four times faster than we can speak. This is how we can multi-task, walk and chew gum at the same time. It is also how something we were trying to remember a few days ago suddenly pops into our head out of nowhere.

Have you ever forgotten someone's name or title of a movie? You can't think of it and tell yourself that you'll think of it later. When you do remember, it's while you're doing something completely unrelated. You weren't even thinking about it, but for some reason the name or title popped into your mind out of nowhere. Well, that is your subconscious mind at work. It never rests. It is always at work.

The subconscious is where all of our emotion and creativity is stored, but we rarely tap into it. Often times, we avoid it. I believe if we harness the power of our subconscious we can help manifest our dreams to create a better life for ourselves. My coaching certification is in Subconscious Restructuring as more and more research continues to uncover how much our subconscious drives all of our behavior.

Psychologist, Joseph M. Carver Ph.D. helps us understand how "Emotional Memory Management (EMM)" enables us to manage our emotions in a way that will produce more POSITIVE outcomes for us. The key, of course, is managing how we RESPOND to our emotions.

We all know what memory is, but in the past we thought this memory simply contained data much like a computer maintains a system of files. New studies in psychology and neurology now tell us that the files not only contain data and information, but emotions as well. In a manner that is still not fully understood, our brain stores the emotions of an experience as they occurred at the time the memory was made.

As a result, memory files contain two parts: the information about the event and the feeling we had at the time the event occurred. Therefore, when we remember an event, we experience the same feelings we had at the time of the event. It is critical we understand how this impacts our behavior and the choices we make.

We experience a variety of emotions throughout a typical day. A specific area of the brain will hold memories for about five days. After this period, memories that are not important are typically erased and will never be recovered. A memory is important if it has a strong emotional impact on you and will hence be stored in your brain. Over time, we create a large file system of memories that consist of both positive and negative emotions.

Our brain pulls these memory files constantly without us even realizing it. According to Carver's research, our brain has the ability to pull memory files both on purpose and by accident. The good news here is that we can control what memory file we pull by selecting our thoughts. Perhaps even better news is the newfound knowledge that the brain only allows one emotional file out at a time.

According to Carver's research, the brain will focus on anything we choose, which means that we can choose which emotional file or tape we want to play. Even more significant, in my opinion, is the fact that the brain will only allow one emotional file or tape to play at a time. This means, if you decide to pull a different emotional file, your brain will completely go along with that idea.

Carver explains that the brain doesn't care which file is active. He compares it to breathing and explains that the brain operates in automatic just like when we breathe. It will automatically pull files throughout our day, just like breathing occurs without having to focus on it. However, in the same way that we can control our breathing by slowing down our inhale and exhale, we can also control our emotions by controlling what memory file we select.

When the brain operates in automatic, the files it pulls are influenced by our mood. Therefore, if you are depressed and your brain is on automatic, it will pull negative files that reinforce this mood. The key finding in this research is the discovery that we have the ability to change our mood or attitude by choosing which emotional file we pull.

As my best friend and very wise mother always says:

"Make it a great day or not. The choice is yours!"

Positive Thinking

The power of positive thinking is huge. We have heard it all before, but I would like to expand on why I believe this to be true. I'm sure you have heard the saying, 'We are what we eat,' right? Well, I also believe that 'we are what we think.' If we choose to think positive thoughts, our lives will evolve accordingly. If we choose to think negative thoughts, a cycle of negativity will result.

Please understand that you have the ability to influence the direction of your thoughts. I view depression as anger turned inward, which is a direct result of years of uninterrupted negative thinking patterns. The key is to INTERRUPT the negative patterns of thinking by replacing them with positive thoughts. Sounds pretty simple, doesn't it? Well, it is, but it does take time and dedication.

Depression develops over time so it may go without saying that it can take the same amount of time to recover from depression and break the pattern of negative thinking. The brain can heal itself after trauma, but it requires time. You can break the negative patterns of thinking by forcing your brain to strengthen other areas of your brain that are not related to memories of your toxic relationship.

If we think positively, endorphins and other pleasure-related substances are released, which strengthens a positive feedback cycle of thought, rather than negative. In this way, we do have the power to retrain our brain.

The knowledge that we can restore our brain's capacity to engage in healthy thinking patterns again is very reassuring. We must remember that anxiety is something we all experience. We cannot avoid it. The key is learning how to RESPOND to anxiety.

"Learn to select your thoughts the same way you select your clothes every day. Now that's a power that you can cultivate." **-Richard in "Eat, Pray & Love"**

Doing something positive to manage anxiety is a healthy coping strategy. Practicing different methods of relaxation is an effective means of managing anxiety. Listed below are additional ways we can retrain our body and mind to respond to anxiety in a manner that is healthy and productive.

Create

One way to break negative patterns of thinking is to create something or start a new hobby. The more challenging the better because you want to occupy more resources in your brain towards learning something new rather than thinking about the past. When you are not actively thinking about your narcissist, the neuronal networks in your brain related to negative memories are not being strengthened. We can alter our own thought processes by using very simple methods and exercises.

Creativity allows us to express our emotions in a way nothing else can. Now that you no longer avoid feeling, start to celebrate the power of your emotions by expressing yourself creatively.

Dr. Stephen Diamond says creativity "is one of humankind's healthiest inclinations, one of our greatest attributes," and explains that our impulse to be creative "can be understood to some degree as the subjective struggle to give form, structure and constructive expression to inner and outer chaos and conflict."

Create your own prescription for promoting happiness. Whether you write poetry, paint, make pottery and crafts, knit, choreograph a dance, perform in a play, compose a song or simply put pen to paper to write something, to create makes us feel good.

Exercise

Exercise has been linked to positive mental health in numerous studies. Physical movement of the body releases feel-good brain chemicals (neurotransmitters and endorphins) that ease depression and lift our overall mood. Exercise reduces immune system chemicals that can worsen depression. It increases our body temperature, which has a calming effect.

Next time you're feeling anxiety, cope in a healthy way and choose to respond by working out and getting physically active. Research on anxiety tells us that the physical and psychological benefits of exercise can help reduce anxiety and improve mood.

Psychologically, exercise helps you gain confidence by challenging you to meet goals. Getting in shape makes you feel better about your appearance. Working out is a wonderful distraction that can get you away from the cycle of negative thoughts that feed anxiety and depression.

By exercising, you can take your mind off your worries and give yourself time to think about how to respond to anxiety in the most productive manner. Remember, we all experience anxiety. The key is learning how to RESPOND to it. Exercise can also help anxiety and depression from coming back once you're feeling better.

Music

Whether I play it, sing along or dance to it, music is like food for my soul. One of the best ways I have found to stop my brain from getting stuck in negative patterns of thinking is to turn on or play my favorite music.

"Music is the movement of sound to reach the soul for the education of its virtue." **-Plato**

The type of music that helps one person relax may be completely different from what helps another person relax. Whatever your preference, research shows that music significantly reduces anxiety and nervous system arousal.[4]

The body responds to rhythmic, soothing movement. This is why yoga has become such a popular form of exercise and explains why people enjoy dancing so much. Moving your body to a beat is extremely calming and enjoyable.

"In music the passions enjoy themselves." **-Friedrich Nietzsche**

I spent one winter cutting an album with some friends in a studio in Chicago. We recorded 10 cover songs by my favorite female vocalists.

I co-wrote one song with William Ellis and Robin Grant of Nashville. Without a doubt, it was the most cathartic experience of my life. I never promoted it or intended to launch a singing career from it, but it helped me process my pain in a way that was truly liberating.

https://music.apple.com/us/album/gotta-get-it-out/316448797

Breathing Techniques

I'm sure you have heard that taking quick shallow breaths increases your anxiety. The reason for this is because short breaths signal to the brain that a threat exists, which automatically stimulates a stress response that leads to destructive patterns of thinking. On the other hand, taking deep breaths tells your brain all is well and allows you to relax.

"There are over two thousand organs and hormones that can be affected positively or negatively in a manner of minutes by shifting your breathing patterns," states Dr. Frank Lawlis. One model of breathing I have found to be very effective when responding to anxiety is what Dr. Lawlis refers to as *Circle Breath*:

The idea is to keep a steady exchange of air inhaling and exhaling, creating a circle of airflow through the lungs. This should be done in a relaxed manner utilizing imagery. When inhaling, you should imagine positive and nurturing air entering your body and mind. While exhaling, you should think about releasing all the inner toxins and negative patterns of thinking into the air. Essentially, you are inhaling positive vibrations while exhaling toxic energy.[5]

Meditation

Meditation has been practiced since ancient times as a component of numerous religious traditions and has recently gained a great deal of empirical evidence to support its effectiveness.

According to Wikipedia, "Over 1000 published research studies support the fact that various methods of meditation have been linked to changes in metabolism, blood pressure, brain activation, and other bodily processes. Meditation has been used in clinical settings as a method of stress and pain reduction."

The aim of meditation is to bring inner peace within our self by changing our thoughts from negative to positive. By focusing within our self and tapping into our spirituality, we learn to transform and nurture the natural qualities within. Meditation is a self-healing process. The person who meditates gains a wonderful sense of their true self.

I recently became certified in Mindfulness and find it to be incredibly helpful to managing my anxiety. Meditation allows your mind to settle inward beyond thought to experience the source of thought – known as true consciousness, mindfulness or pure awareness. In this state, we are most in touch with our innermost self and feel most at peace.

"Within you there is a stillness and a sanctuary to which you can retreat at any time and be yourself." -Hermann Hesse

During meditation, we must allow ourselves to simply be and not fill in the space with outside noise or distraction. We must learn not to impulsively fill the empty space with our usual compulsions. Learning how to meditate is truly transformative for when we have seen ourselves completely, we no longer get jumpy or restless or need to keep busy. A thoroughly good relationship with oneself results in being able to be still in silence.

Massage

Our bodies are hardwired to need touch, but I don't recommend jumping into a new romantic relationship right away. You need to take time for yourself to heal. Therefore, get a massage from a professional or buy something you can use to massage yourself. The act of touch and massage releases endorphins and neurotransmitters like serotonin making you feel better physically and emotionally. Treat yourself to a massage or hot bath. You will be amazed at how much it relaxes you and reduces your anxiety.

Connect with Others

I believe we are all inter-connected. It is especially important during recovery to reach out to others. We only hurt ourselves when we disconnect or withdraw. Humans cannot thrive in isolation. When we connect with others we discover our kinship with one another. We realize we are not alone and others can relate to our pain. Our struggle seems less insurmountable because we have others who understand what we're going through. Talking to others who can relate is the best form of therapy I have ever found, which is precisely why I created our support group.

Give Back to Others

Helping others is rewarding and fulfilling. I am dedicated to building awareness on the devastating effects of being in a relationship with a narcissist. I enjoy finding opportunities to give back and help others. There are many ways to do this and I encourage you to identify how you can give back in a way that is unique to you.

"The best way to find yourself is to lose yourself in the service of others." -Mahatma Gandhi

Celebrate Your Success

Positive reinforcement is necessary in order to implement any long-term change. Thanks to science we now know that retraining the brain is possible, but keep in mind the brain must experience positive reinforcement in order to fully integrate any significant change. We must enjoy what we are doing in order to continue doing it. If one coping strategy does not work for you, do not force yourself to continue it. Try another method. Everyone is different and what works for one person may not work for someone else. Keep trying until you find a strategy that you truly enjoy and can embrace. Celebrate success at every opportunity. Positive reinforcement must occur if any of these changes are going to last.

There is no overnight cure to repairing the damage caused by long-term emotional abuse and trauma in a relationship. If anyone tells you otherwise, please be cautious. In my opinion, any program that promises to fix you overnight or in a few quick sessions is exploiting you. The key to any learning is repetition, time, practice and steadfast commitment.

The power to change is yours and yours alone. No one can take this gift from you, but you must treat it as a gift. Never take it for granted. Harness it and take control of this miraculous power you possess.

Learning how to cope with anxiety in a healthy way will allow you to start living and feeling again. Believe me when I tell you, I am living proof that it is possible to retrain your brain so you can stop negative obsessive patterns of thinking and start living life.

We now know it is possible to teach the brain to react in certain ways in situations in the same manner as it is possible to teach the body to move in new ways through physical therapy. I believe this information is all we need to know in order to rest assured that we will heal from these toxic relationships.

CHAPTER 6

SELF-CARE

We must lighten up, relax and go easy on ourselves. Many of us find it easy to have compassion for others, but have very little for ourselves. It never occurs to us to feel it for ourselves. Living life with an unconditional love for ourselves changes everything. We get rid of the 'should haves' and the 'could haves' and gradually discover ourselves by being honest and staying in the moment. Without any agenda except for being real, we begin to find ourselves again. We assume responsibility for being here in this messy world and realize how precious life is.

I am often asked when the grieving ends. Everyone is different. You can't put a time frame on the healing process. What I do know is that the longer you avoid your pain, the longer it takes to recover. We must confront our pain and process it in order to heal and move on. As we discussed, writing about it helps, expressing ourselves helps, meditating helps. All of these things help, but it is up to you to put these things in motion for yourself.

By learning from the moments in life, we become more compassionate and can aspire to live in the now. We can relax and open our heart and mind to what is right in front of us in the moment. We see, feel and experience everything more vividly. This is living. Now is the time to experience enlightenment. Not some time in the future. Keep in mind, how we relate to the now creates the future.

"Nothing we can do can change the past, but everything we do changes the future." -Ashleigh Brilliant

When we find ourselves in a mess, we don't have to feel guilty about it and angry. Instead, we should reflect on the fact that how we RESPOND to the situation determines whatever happens next for us. We can become depressed and cynical or we can look at it as an opportunity to make ourselves strong. It is all a choice. Being brave enough to be fully alive and awake every moment of life, including the dark times, is to truly experience life to its fullest.

Eckhart Tolle explains that each of us has a voice in our head that reminds us of troubles from our past and also encourages us to worry about our future. Some individuals listen to this voice more than others. Certain events or experiences can cause this voice in our head to run incessantly. We know unresolved trauma leads to obsessive thoughts.

Tolle helps us understand that all negativity is caused by too much focus on the past or future. He explains that worry and anxiety are caused by too much future focus and not enough presence. Being stuck in the past, either feeling resentful or guilty, is a result of too much past and not enough presence. By focusing on the past or future and denying the reality of your present, you remain stuck. Identification with your mind causes thought to be compulsive. Tolle explains that this mental noise prevents you from finding the realm of inner stillness inside you that is necessary to achieve enlightenment.[1]

Since the beginning of time, spiritual teachers of all traditions have pointed to the *Now* as the key to enlightenment. Meditation is one way you can learn to live in the moment and I highly recommend you explore it. It takes time to learn to stay focused on the present, and you may need to try more than one method before finding one that works for you, but please don't give up. It is easy to get distracted by time, noise, anxiety and fear. However, learning how to live in the moment is worth every bit of effort. Once you know how to do it, it is truly life-changing.

When you realize that all of our anxiety in life comes from:

REGRETTING THE PAST or WORRYING ABOUT THE FUTURE

it helps focus on the present moment. The present truly is a gift to be cherished. An *attitude of gratitude* can change your life. If you stop in the moment and ask yourself if you're ok, you realize you are not starving, you are not oppressed and you are not a prisoner of war somewhere. You are in a safe place and have much to be grateful for in life.

You must have self-compassion for yourself right now in order to heal. We must forgive ourselves entirely for any part we played in continuing the relationship we had with an emotionally abusive person. You have done nothing wrong, but believe in the goodness of another person. Please do not beat yourself up for a poor choice, but instead forgive yourself and use the knowledge gained to never allow it to happen again.

Honor Your Anger

Many of us were taught to repress anger. Anger has a negative connotation because most people associate it with aggression. But in reality, anger is followed by violence only 10 percent of the time, according to Howard Kassinove, PH.D., co-author of "Anger Management: The Compete Treatment Guide for Practice."

Many of us are conditioned to feel shame for feeling any feelings of anger. Anger runs deep. We may have feelings of anger, but we refuse to acknowledge these feelings. We must feel our feelings in order to heal. It is ok to be angry about how we were treated in the past. We must acknowledge and honor our feelings. We are entitled to feel the way we do.

We may not only feel shame, but in the case of our narcissist, we simply do not want to face the truth. To face the truth means we have to make changes in our life that will not be easy. It takes courage to get real. I know I buried my head in the sand for years in my marriage. I did not want to admit that my marriage was not working. It is simply easier to deny things sometimes. However, to deny our feelings is to deny our true self and is no way to live.

Used productively, anger can help us restore our self-esteem and exert more control over our lives. Processing our anger is absolutely critical to our recovery. However, we must be careful in how we process it. As mentioned, anger is neither a positive or negative emotion. How we RESPOND and REACT to anger is what makes all the difference in the world.

The key is not to avoid anger, the key is to learn how to RESPOND to anger.

The idea of constructive anger is gaining a great deal of empirical support lately. Research tells us that processing our anger in productive ways leads to health benefits. Experts say that constructive anger can improve intimate and work relationships.

It is one thing to stay silent when you disagree with someone or something, but quite another to simply allow others to walk all over you. Some of you may just be starting to realize what an abusive relationship you were really in. I would guarantee that feelings of anger and resentment towards your significant other are what finally caused you to see the light and take action. Anger is a natural defense mechanism designed to protect us from abuse. We should never deny our feelings of anger, but honor them.

Anger like all feelings is a normal, healthy and essential emotion. Getting angry does not make you a bad person. Anger is a biological safeguard to ensure our survival. Anger is our body's response to internal or external demands, threats and pressures. Anger warns us that there is a problem or a potential threat. At the same time, it gives us courage to face the problem or meet the threat by providing us with a release of the hormone adrenaline.

Adrenaline prepares us to meet the threat by raising our defenses and giving us a boost of energy. This in turn provides us with added strength to fight off our enemy or added speed in which to run from the enemy. Think of Darwin's survival of the fittest theory. We should never ignore our emotions. They exist for a reason: to warn us, protect us and guide us through life.

Cruel behavior or abusive remarks from others should not be tolerated. We have a right to be angry when someone hurts or insults us. It is a threat to our emotional well-being. Anger is the emotion that alerts us that something is wrong and causes us to finally take action.

"What happens is not as important as how you react to what happens." -Thaddeus Gola

Do not hide from your anger. You must recognize it as a signal that there is a problem that needs to be resolved. We become angry because there is an issue of some kind that requires our attention. In my opinion, anger is like an internal alarm system telling us something is wrong. To ignore it is dangerous.

Research tells us people who do not acknowledge anger or do not process anger in a healthy way are more vulnerable to health problems. Rates of diagnosed cancer are found to be higher in those who have never openly expressed their anger.

"Holding on to anger is like grasping a hot coal with the intent of throwing it at someone else; You are the one who gets burned." **-Buddha**

Do not repress your anger. Acknowledging your anger is the first step in releasing resentment and ultimately allows you to move on. Forgiveness is a personal choice each of us should make. Everyone's situation is different. I can't advise on whether one should forgive their abuser. On the other hand, I do think it is critical we forgive ourselves for falling for someone who wasn't who we thought they were. We must not beat ourselves up for the time we spent in a toxic relationship. We did absolutely nothing wrong but believe in the goodness of another human being. Forgiving ourselves is essential.

Hopefully, you're beginning to see the importance of acknowledging and processing your feelings of anger when they occur. If we do not allow ourselves to feel anger, we lose out on the benefits of it, such as motivation, strength, energy, power and protection.

Many of us do not realize just how powerful a force anger can be. When anger is used to motivate us to make life changes that promote our emotional well-being, it is positive. However, when we express anger through aggressive or passive-aggressive means, it is negative.

Anger can motivate you to make needed changes in your life or it can make you emotionally and physically ill if you hold it in. It can empower you or it can kill your relationships if you take your anger out on someone in the wrong way. Instead of being honest and acknowledging their anger, many people shift blame, project and abuse others.

"It's not the load that breaks you down, it's the way you carry it." -Lena Horne

I believe the way you handle your anger affects all of your relationships, including your relationship with yourself. Many of us are so afraid of anger that we direct the anger inward at ourselves instead of expressing it outward. Others take their anger out on innocent people. Anger externalized can lead to violence, while anger internalized causes depression and health problems.

Why is it that we feel there are only two responses to anger – to blame others or blame ourselves? Why does someone always have to be right and someone else have to be wrong? Thinking in black and white terms like this closes us down and makes our world smaller. Wanting things to fit in a perfect little box is futile. We will only find ourselves banging our head against the wall in frustration instead of learning from the experience. If we allow ourselves to learn from the disagreement, we may realize there are much needed changes we need to make in our life.

If your narcissist cheated on you, you may try to blame the person she had an affair with and focus your anger there. However, it is important to recognize that by blaming someone else, you are denying the truth about the reality of your situation. Instead of dealing with the fact that the person you love cheated on you, you are wasting time being mad at someone else.

This just keeps us stuck and will only slow down our recovery process. Until we can acknowledge who we are really angry at, we will never work through our feelings so we can move on. At the end of the day, we must look at our relationship, deal with the reality of it and get honest with ourselves in order to move on.

As you know by now, I believe life is all about how we RESPOND to it. We need to open our minds and heart to stay in the uncertainty where we don't need to define who is right or who is wrong in every situation. It doesn't matter. What matters is what you learn from it. What is your experience? This is living. This is open space. Everything is ambiguous and always changing, shifting. Finding absolute right and wrong is a trick we play on ourselves to think we're in control. We think it helps us feel safe and secure.

Unfortunately, it does the opposite. It makes us more uneasy because we know we're lying to ourselves. Subconsciously, we know this. Instead of lying or hiding from the truth, we must be compassionate with ourselves. We tell ourselves we want unconditional love from another person, yet we can't even give it to ourselves. Instead of acknowledging when we are wrong or when we have faults, we lie to ourselves that we are perfect. No one is perfect. To be with someone who unconditionally loves you means they accept you for who you are – they take the good with the bad and they love you unconditionally.

Why can't we do this for ourselves?

Until we can do this for ourselves, we will never live an authentic life. We must be honest and compassionate with ourselves. This is referred to as *loving-kindness* in Buddhism. We must go easy on ourselves to find love for the parts of ourselves that aren't perfect. We must have an unconditional relationship with ourselves. If we can't love ourselves, we cannot expect anyone else to love us.

You will remain in a state of pain, darkness or unhappiness as long as you continue to lie to yourself and deny your reality. You must have a total commitment to reality in order to heal. The more you resist the present moment, the more pain you create within yourself.

We must get to know the nature of our restlessness and fear. It is how we get to know ourselves on the deepest level possible. To live an authentic life, we must get real to heal. Many people are afraid of the truth. However, to finally confront the truth is the most liberating and freeing thing you can do for yourself. It is truly transformative.

Acknowledge Your Fear

What prevents us from looking honestly at our situation? Fear. Whatever we fear controls us. Fear, if not confronted, prevents us from truly living. Fear is like a prison.

"The only thing we have to fear is fear itself." **-F.D. Roosevelt**

Powerful words, right? Well, fear is a very powerful emotion. We live in a society that throws fear in our face at every opportunity. Marketers sell to us by playing on our fear. The government uses fear to control us and keep us complacent. Society encourages us to distract ourselves from fear by numbing ourselves with alcohol, drugs or pills. We are so afraid of fear that it paralyzes us.

Our modern culture has conditioned us to avoid pain and seek pleasure and to think only in terms of dualities or complete opposites. Instead of finding a balance, we are led to believe that everything has to be either:

RIGHT OR WRONG

BLACK OR WHITE

FAIR OR UNFAIR

CERTAIN OR UNCERTAIN

And here's the biggest misconception that ruins our entire view of life:

PLEASURE OR PAIN

Yes, we are conditioned and programmed to think we can:

SEEK PLEASURE AND AVOID PAIN

Everything we do is centered around running from pain and enhancing pleasure. But guess what? Guess what is so fundamentally wrong with this?

We cannot avoid pain. To think we can is ignorant. Yet, many of us spend our lives fooling ourselves to think we can. Suffering is part life. We lie to ourselves that everything is ok when it's not. It is this behavior that keeps us stuck and dead inside.

"Pain and pleasure, like light and darkness, succeed each other."
-Laurence Stern

We must accept that with pleasure comes pain and with pain comes pleasure. We must learn to live in the grey and stop trying to force certainty in life where there can be none. The more we deny our reality and lie to ourselves, the deeper we put ourselves in the dark.

Unfortunately, this is how many of us learned how to get through the tough times. We have learned to use denial as a coping mechanism. What we fail to realize is that the very method we thought was helping us is really killing us inside.

"God instructs the heart not by ideas, but by pains and contradictions." -Jean Pierre De Caussade

When something hurts in life, we typically avoid it. We rarely think of it as something we are meant to learn from. In fact, we immediately try to find a way to get rid of the painful feeling and tell ourselves we will be happy when something else we've been waiting for happens. For example, we tell ourselves when we move into our new home we'll be happy, or when we meet our soul mate, we will be happy. This is no way to go through life. It's a vicious cycle that never ends. We run away thinking we can avoid our reality, but what we don't realize is:

Nothing ever goes away until it has taught us what we need to know.

We can lie to ourselves or run all we want, but the lesson will keep returning in different forms and manifestations until we learn what it is trying to teach us about our reality. The very first noble truth the Buddha points out is that suffering is inevitable in human beings. It is part of the human condition. We cannot avoid it.

We must accept suffering and open our hearts to look at how weak we are being by trying to avoid it. Only then can we discover that the very thing that terrifies us is in fact a way for us to reconnect with our true self. Facing reality shows you who you are and what is true. Facing our fear and waking up tells us something about ourselves. We must get to know fear, become familiar and intimate with it. It teaches us something. When we stop running and don't act out, repress or blame, we encounter our true self.

Fear of the unknown is the cause for most, if not all, anxiety. We do not like uncertainty in life. In fact, we dread it. Yet, nothing in life is certain. I spent years of my life trying to force certainty where there could be none, and it only led to obsessive thought that distracted me from the present moment. We cannot force anything in life. To try to do so is futile

Years ago, my therapist suggested that I learn to *live in the gray* and it has helped me tremendously. It took me some time to adopt this new mindset, but it's been incredibly helpful. *Living in the gray* means to accept that we don't know what's going to happen next in life and that no matter what we do, we cannot control it or predict it. We must accept it. We must accept the gray and stand firm in the knowledge that whatever happens next in life, we have the ability to respond to it. Our response is where our power lies.

"Between stimulus and response there is a space. In that space is our power to choose our response. In our response lies our growth and our freedom." – Victor Frankl

Living in the gray also helps us stop thinking in extremes or splitting (i.e. black and white thinking). Things are not black or white...all good or all bad....perfect or imperfect...right or wrong. They can be somewhere in the middle (i.e. gray), and to be honest, that's really what we should expect. We should never expect perfection. Life is messy.

It wasn't until I accepted that we're not supposed to know what's going to happen next in life that I finally started to thrive. I finally stopped obsessing over the anxiety of what was going to happen next to relax in the moment. By learning to be okay in the gray, we accept uncertainty and become comfortable with it. We allow ourselves to be curious about life and stop letting fear hold us back. Life is a journey into the unknown...an adventure. We must celebrate this and not be afraid of it.

"Fear is the mind-killer. Fear is the little-death that brings total obliteration. I will face my fear. I will permit it to pass over me and through me. And when it has gone past, I will turn the inner eye to see its path. Where the fear has gone, there will be nothing. Only I will remain." –Frank Herbert (Dune)

Life is a journey...an adventure. We must celebrate this and not be afraid of it. Learning to live in the grey means we accept uncertainty in life. I'm not supposed to know what's going to happen next in life, but knowing I have the confidence, mindset and freedom to respond appropriately empowers me.

We must get to know fear and become familiar with fear. Look it right in the eye. In my opinion, it is the only way to undo negative patterns of thinking. If we face something head on, we no longer play mind games with ourselves to avoid it.

When we face fear, we will be humbled. There will be little room for the arrogance of holding onto ideals or lying to ourselves as a method of escaping reality. The kinds of discoveries that are made in painful situations have much to do with having the courage to feel. When we stop and feel our feelings, we encounter our true being. We are more in touch with ourselves than ever before. This is what we call *Mindfulness*. Clarity provides direction. We must never fear the reality of our situation, no matter how overwhelming it may seem.

"We can easily forgive a child who is afraid of the dark: the real tragedy of life is when men are afraid of the light." -Plato

Acceptance

We often upset ourselves as a result of how we choose to RESPOND to life. Most disturbance comes from the belief that we should be able to control others in an attempt to control ourselves. Unfortunately, what we fail to realize is the only person we can control is ourselves.

Instead of focusing on what we cannot change or control, we must focus our efforts on that which we can control. The Serenity Prayer is a wonderful reminder of this:

> God, Grant me the
>
> Serenity to accept the things I cannot change,
>
> Courage to change the things I can, and the
>
> Wisdom to know the difference.

It is how we RESPOND to life that matters. Therefore, it is critical that we understand what we can and cannot control. We have choices in life, and while we cannot control what happens to us, we can control how we RESPOND to it. It is the choices we make after a setback that determine our destiny. My very wise older brother once told me:

"My proudest moments in life are not my achievements, but my ability to bounce off the lows in life. It's the climb and journey from that low that is most rewarding."

Acceptance is critical to begin the climb. In my opinion, until we accept our situation for what it is and all its craziness, we will never move on. We must distinguish what we can control from what we cannot control. This is very important because it really helps us understand what is within our grasp and what is not.

Everything outside of our control is something we must let go of so we can put all of our energy into the areas we can control. Identifying the difference between what we can control and what we cannot is absolutely essential. It helps us succeed in life and stay focused.

The trick is to keep exploring and not bail out, even when we learn something we don't want to accept. Nothing is what we thought. Accepting truth puts you on the spot. At times, accepting truth may cause us to initially suffer. However, this is where we have a choice. We must realize we are on the verge of something. We can choose to shut down and feel resentful, or we can hone in on the throbbing quality of truth. It is a testing of sorts...a testing of our ability to awaken our hearts.

When things feel like they can't get any worse, we have a choice. We may think the point is to pass the test or overcome the problem, but the truth is that some things cannot be solved. They must be accepted. Things come together and fall apart all the time.

The healing comes from allowing these things to happen. Much obsessing comes from trying to control the unknown. Until we accept the fact that we cannot control the unknown, a constant battle will ensue in our minds. The reason for this is because deep down, we know we cannot control everything. To fool ourselves into thinking we can only contributes to our Cognitive Dissonance. We may think something is going to bring us pleasure, but it does not. We may think something is going to bring us misery, but it may not. The truth is, we don't know. We must learn to accept the fact that we don't know what's really going to happen. Allowing ourselves to realize we don't know what is going to happen is the most healing lesson of all. After all, life is a journey. As long as we stay mindful and are honest with ourselves, we have the strength to face what life may bring us.

Running away is like preferring death to life. We may be in the dark right now, but from darkness comes light. If we commit ourselves to feeling our emotions and staying right where we are, our experience becomes vivid. Things become very clear when we don't try to escape or run from them.

"One's action ought to come out of an achieved stillness: not to be mere rushing on." -D. H. Lawrence

Whatever arises, we must not judge. We must not avoid. We must use everything that happens to us as a means for waking up. We must reverse our habitual pattern of trying to avoid pain by allowing ourselves to feel the moment and understand what it is we are meant to learn from it. We must stop looking for alternatives and cheat ourselves of the present moment.

Unlike the narcissist, engaging the ego is an OPTION for us. We must remember to let go of our ego and discipline ourselves not to escape reality. Instead, we must practice acceptance. The ego always feels threatened and always lives in a state of fear and want. Once you understand this, you must step out of it so you can face your fear and surrender your ego. When we do not run, we discover our innermost essence. Whatever arises, we do not judge. Give up the idea that pain can be avoided and have the courage to relax with the reality of your situation. Commit to staying in the moment. Things become very clear when there is nowhere to escape. To accept uncertainty and stay with it is the path to true awakening.

Embrace the moment and be open to what you are supposed to learn from it. Wake up and allow yourself to experience pain. It is a fundamental part of life. We think by protecting ourselves from suffering we are being kind to ourselves. This could not be further from the truth. In fact, by doing this we are only becoming more fearful. This alienates us and hardens us. We disconnect from ourselves without even realizing it. If we shield ourselves from discomfort, we will suffer.

Many people never let their guard down to love another person because they are so afraid of getting hurt. Those who live with a guarded heart are not living. They are merely existing and their existence is a sad one.

"It is better to have loved and lost than never to have loved at all." -Alfred Lord Tennyson

We must wake up and let go of our ego. We must find a balance between thinking everything has to be defined as either all good or all bad. As we discussed earlier, black and white thinking is toxic. We must learn to live in the grey. Acknowledging that life is messy and never perfect is the first step to waking up and living in the moment. It allows us to discover our innermost essence. We must learn how to allow ourselves to stay in the moment and connect with the richness of it, the rawness of it, the tenderness of it and the pain of it.

"All the world is full of suffering. It is also full of overcoming." **-Helen Keller**

When we don't close off and let our hearts break, we not only find ourselves, but we discover our kinship with all beings. This is why our support group is so powerful. Connecting with others on a level no one else can and in a manner that is so raw and real is life-changing. Together, we help each other face the truth. Yes, it can be difficult but at the same time, it's absolutely essential in order to heal and move on. To me, this is the essence of waking up. *Bochichista* is a Buddhist term for a noble or awakened heart and describes this process beautifully.

To try to avoid pain and suffering is to live a false existence. It is a lie to tell yourself you can avoid pain. To fend off how we feel only hardens us. We should not be afraid to feel. We should not be ashamed of the love and grief it invokes in us. I would rather feel pain and know I'm alive than feel nothing. We must take it all in. Let the pain of the world touch your heart and turn it into compassion for yourself and others.

Learning not to run away or lie to ourselves about our reality takes time. Running away is so deep-seated in us. We are conditioned so that the minute things get tough or we even think things are going to get tough, we run. The trick is to avoid running and commit to the moment….to stay there and deal with it. Instead of manipulating the situation or lying to ourselves, we allow ourselves to be with it and understand what we are meant to learn from it.   It starts by learning to love ourselves unconditionally.

Have a Love Affair with Yourself

If you're reading this book, you are most likely an *Empath*, which we discussed earlier. This means you have an intense feeling of empathy and compassion for others and it makes you feel good to take care of others. However, please do not rush into another relationship because of this instinct. Instead, channel it inward towards yourself. You need to take care of yourself for a change. You need to practice self-care and self-compassion.

Although taking care of yourself will feel foreign at first, it is the best thing you can do for yourself right now. You must spend time alone before jumping into a new relationship. You need to find yourself again. You should not rush into a new relationship. You need to enjoy the benefits of being alone. You owe it to yourself.

We spend way too much time trying to form and nurture relationships with others who could potentially be our soul mate, when the whole time we neglect to nurture and get to know ourselves. It is time to have a love affair with yourself!

"To love oneself is the beginning of a life-long romance." **-Oscar Wilde**

You are finally living in the light and moving away from the darkness. It is time to connect with yourself again. Being in touch with yourself and your true emotions is truly a gift that we all must cherish and embrace.

The Hidden Benefits of Struggle

As he says in his famous book "Man's Search for Meaning":

"Suffering ceases to be suffering the moment it finds a meaning." **-Victor Frankl**

This couldn't be more true, in my opinion. I know that had I not experienced what I did, I would not know myself the way I do now. Had certain events not forced me to look deep inside myself for strength, I would still be sleeping through life.

We must use everything that happens to us as a means for waking up. No one should feel shame for hard times. Suffering is part of life. The sooner we accept this, the better.

Stop avoiding pain and seeking only pleasure. Instead, start discovering the fundamental meaning behind the things we experience.

"We can discover meaning in life in three different ways:

(1) by creating a work or doing a deed; (2) by experiencing something or encountering someone; and (3) by the attitude we take toward unavoidable suffering." **-Victor Frankl**

Struggle toughens the human spirit and strengthens our character. It gives us purpose and direction. Following the path of least resistance in life is a cop-out. It is struggle and pain that leads to transformation.

This idea has changed many people's attitude towards suffering and I hope it changes yours as well. As you experience the pain of losing your narcissist, use it to empower you to discover the real meaning behind your relationship. I truly believe every relationship is meant to teach us something in life. Think about what you learned from this relationship. Things can be better for you not despite your suffering but because of it.

"What doesn't kill us makes us stronger." -Friedrich Nietzsche

<u>**Moving Forward**</u>

To live in denial and avoidance is to prefer death over life. Others may have lied to us for years, but to lie to ourselves is no longer acceptable. It is no way to live. You can't run from yourself, avoid your feelings, or deny your reality for any longer. No one who is lying to themselves is living in the light of consciousness.

Enlightenment is what we all seek, but in order to achieve this, we first must be honest with ourselves about our situation. We cannot avoid anger and fear. Anger and fear can motivate you to make necessary changes in your life. We must feel these feelings, confront them and process them before we can truly move on.

We should never be afraid to ask for support from others in our quest to evolve. I believe we are all interconnected. If we need to heal, we must reach out to others. People only hurt themselves when they disconnect or withdraw from others. Being afraid to ask for help only leads to further isolation. Humans cannot thrive in isolation. Do not endure this alone. Reach out to a family member, friend, mental health professional or join our support group.

Please do not close yourself off from others because you have been hurt. You were born giving and receiving love and you are still capable of loving in every way that is humanly possible. Embrace your ability to feel love and compassion. When you allow yourself to be your authentic self and love yourself unconditionally, you begin to truly live the life you're meant to live and thrive.

Remember that every day is a gift and every day you wake up, you have a choice. A choice about whether you want to tap into your positive energy or wallow in negative energy. Happiness is a choice we all have and my hope for you is that you choose it every day. You deserve nothing less.

"When I was five years old, my mom told me that happiness was the key to life. When I went to school, they asked me what I wanted to be when I grew up. I wrote down "happy." They told me I didn't understand the assignment. I told them they didn't understand life." -John Lennon

Amazon Book Reviews

NOTES

Introduction

1. Jean M. Twenge and W. Keith Campbell, "The Narcissism Epidemic – Living in the Age of Entitlement" (New York: Free Press/Simon &Schuster, 2009).

Chapter 1

1. Sam Vaknin, "Malignant Self-Love – Narcissism Revisited" (Prague: Narcissus Publications, 2006).
2. Ibid.

Chapter 2

1. Louise DeSalvo, "Writing as Way of Healing – How Telling Our Stories Transforms Our Lives" (Boston: Beacon Press, 1999), p. 43.
2. Eckhart Tolle, "The Power of Now" (Vancouver, BC: Namestate Publishing, 1999).

Chapter 5

1. Dr. Frank Lawlis, *Retraining the Brain* (New York: Penguin Books, 2009).
2. Ibid.
3. Fred Penzel, *Obsessive-Compulsive Disorders* (New York: Oxford University Press, 2000).
4. Lawlis, *Retraining the Brain.*
5. Ibid.

Chapter 6

1. Eckhart Tolle, *The Power of Now* (Vancouver, BC: Namestate Publishing, 1999).

ABOUT THE AUTHOR

Lisa E. Scott is an HR representative for a global professional services firm and an Adjunct Professor at Loyola University in Chicago. She has four coaching certifications, including her most recent certification in Mindfulness. To engage her coaching services, please use the QR code below:

Printed in Great Britain
by Amazon

41945543R00116